CREATIVITY

A Series of Books in Psychology

Editors:

Richard C. Atkinson
Gardner Lindzey
Richard F. Thompson

CREATIVITY

GENIUS AND OTHER MYTHS

Robert Weisberg
Temple University

 W. H. Freeman and Company
New York

Library of Congress Cataloging-in-Publication Data

Weisberg, Robert W.
  Creativity: genius and other myths.

  (A Series of books in psychology)
  Bibliography: p.
  Includes index.
  1. Creativity ability. I. Title. II. Series.
BF408.W386 1986   153.3′5   86-4263
ISBN 0-7167-1768-9
ISBN 0-7167-1769-7 (pbk.)

Printed in the United States of America.

1 2 3 4 5 6 7 8 9 0 MP 4 3 2 1 0 8 9 8 7 6

To Nancy, Michael, and Rebecca

CONTENTS

ACKNOWLEDGMENTS

Many individuals have contributed to this book. Nora Newcombe and David Goldstein read the entire manuscript in various forms, and provided helpful criticism at many stages. They and Lynn Hasher have been constant sources of stimulation over the years. Sam Glucksberg and Richard Mayer also provided thoughtful reviews of the manuscript. Others whose influence can be discerned here include Tom Busse, Mason Spencer, and Marie DiCamillo. Dorothy Mewha and Cheryl Jones at the Temple Word Processing Center did their usual excellent job of turning rough drafts into a polished manuscript. Finally, Buck Rogers, Stephen Wagley, and their colleagues at W. H. Freeman made the actual production of the book almost a pleasant experience.

Robert Weisberg

CREATIVITY

1

CREATIVITY AND MYTH

The Myth of Creativity

Our society holds a very romantic view about the origins of creative achievements in the arts and sciences. This is the genius view, and at its core is the belief that creative achievements come about through great leaps of imagination which occur because creative individuals are capable of extraordinary thought processes. In addition to their intellectual capacities, creative individuals are assumed to possess extraordinary personality characteristics which also play a role in bringing about creative leaps. These intellectual and personality characteristics are what is called "genius," and they are brought forth as the explanation for great creative achievements.

An example of the genius view is the portrayal of the composer Wolfgang Amadeus Mozart in Peter Shaffer's film *Amadeus*. Vulgar, ill-mannered, immature, spoiled, and childish, Mozart spends too much time drinking and partying, and he is constantly in debt. And yet, he produces the most marvelous music, supposedly without even thinking about it. When the time is right, the music starts to flow, and Mozart simply writes it down. The central character in *Amadeus* is Antonio Salieri, a well-known composer of Mozart's time, who is driven to despair by the superiority of Mozart's music to his own. When Mozart's wife Constanza appeals to Salieri behind Mozart's back to help her husband get a position as music tutor to the Emperor's niece, she brings him Mozart's latest work to demonstrate his capacity as a composer. On examining the manuscripts, Salieri asks Constanza if she is sure that these are manuscripts which Mozart has just been working on. Since they show no deletions or corrections, all this great music must flow already completed from Mozart. The only way in which Salieri can understand how "this creature" could produce such music without mistakes is to assume that Mozart is a messenger of God; obviously, since God is writing the music, there would be no corrections. For some unfathomable reason, God has chosen to express his voice through Mozart (and not through Salieri).

Thus, the messenger of God view assumes that creative products come about through leaps. The creative person suddenly begins to produce something complete without knowing where it is coming from. This view has come down to us at least from the Greeks, who believed that the gods or the Muses breathed creative ideas into the artist. (This is why we say that we get *inspired* when we have a good idea, since inspiration comes from the Latin for *breathe in*.) They accordingly called on the Muses, the nine daughters of Zeus who ruled over the arts and sciences, for inspiration before beginning work.

Some creative artists still talk as if the gods give us creative ideas. In an article in *The New York Times,* the poet Anthony Hecht was quoted as saying "The muse has been with me and collaborating with great fervor." Though this view is no longer widely believed, the idea is advanced that the unconscious mind presents the conscious mind with creative ideas which the conscious person just puts to use. As in the view that the Muses provide us with ideas, our conscious mental processes do little of the real creative work. The assumption is once again that we make a sudden creative leap without being consciously aware of how it came about. Studies of famous scientists and artists often emphasize the spontaneous, "Aha!" aspect of creativity. When they give after-the-fact reports about how they produced an important piece of work, they often emphasize that they solved problems suddenly, with the solution making an unexpected appearance in consciousness.

A second assumption of the genius view is that creative individuals possess some indefinable quality which accounts for how they do the great things they do. According to an article in *The New York Times,* Shakespeare scholars still dispute the authorship of Shakespeare's plays, questioning how one not-very-well-educated actor could have written those great works. One scholar answered this question very simply: "Genius—which can never be explained," and went on to mention that the same answer could apply to Mozart.

In a less romantic way perhaps, a similar view was expressed recently in an article in *Science Digest,* a magazine which presents discussions of scientific topics for nonspecialists. The article, entitled "The Genius Mind," concerned the characteristics that make creative scientists different from ordinary individuals. About the mind of the scientific genius, the author writes: "Its special kind of creativity enables its owner to find significance in the irrelevant and to make meaning from contradictions." Thus, somehow the creative genius is able to make something out of what other people see as nothing.

There is another way of looking at creativity, quite different from the genius view, which we might call the "nothing new" view. This second view, which can be traced back to John Watson, one of the leaders in the development of behaviorism in the United States, tries to remove the mystery by arguing that nothing that a person ever does is truly creative. Watson argued that what seemed to be creative responses were the result of one of two processes. On the one hand, a new situation might be similar to some old situation. Since the "new" situation contains elements that are familiar, these familiar elements serve as the basis for *generalizing* one's old response to the new situation. Therefore, in such a case, the new situation is not really new; it is simply some old situation in a new costume. On the other hand, if the new situation were not similar to some old situation (that is, if the new situation were truly novel), then according to Watson the person would behave *randomly,* combining various responses in all sorts of ways. So, for example, a poet produced a new poem by randomly combining words until something acceptable was accidentally produced.

For the behaviorist, creativity need not be studied or explained because there is no creativity in the sense of some specific process involved in producing something truly new. Either the product is really something old, or a new product is produced by accident.

Defining Creativity.   This book takes a path somewhere in between the genius and the behaviorist views. Creativity is not nearly as mysterious as the genius view leads us to believe, but neither is it as trivial as the behaviorist view claims.

If we adopt either the genius view or the behaviorist view, we are left with the feeling that the scientific study of creative thinking is doomed to failure. If creative achievements do indeed come about through great leaps of insight, brought about by extraordinary thought processes, in individuals who possess some unanalyzable quality called genius, then little more can be said. Creative thinking must remain mysterious and unknowable. My purpose in this book is to dispel some of the romance and mystery surrounding creativity by showing that many of the "facts"—some of which were just outlined—which the genius view assumes are true are not facts at all. They are really more like myths, stories not based on fact which attempt to explain some natural phenomena. In the case of creative thinking, the myths explain the phenomena, the creative products of artists and scientists, by emphasizing unconscious thought processes, far-ranging leaps of insight, and some unique personal characteristics. One purpose of this book is to demonstrate that much of what we believe about creativity is not based on hard data but is more or less folklore, passed down from one generation to the next as if it were the truth. When we see that there is little reason to take these myths seriously, much of the mystery surrounding creativity will disappear. A second purpose of the book is to present a framework for understanding creativity based on experimental results, which can replace the myths.

The discussion will begin with an example of a creative solution to a simple real-life problem, and a look at laboratory research examining creative problem solving. These will serve as the basis for some general statements about the production of creative solutions to problems. This will lead to a critical examination of the traditional literature on creative thinking, particularly the evidence for the widely held view that creativity depends on unconscious processes, that these unconscious processes produce far-ranging leaps of imagination, and that creative geniuses are different from ordinary people. The creative capacity that the ancient Greeks assigned to the mythical gods has in our era been assigned to the unconscious and to other exotic processes. The evidence I will discuss will show that the modern view is no less a myth.

Problem Solving

It is very difficult to discuss creativity because it means very different things to people. I have heard the term used to refer to problem solving, artistic work, scientific work, divorce ("creative divorce"), and retirement. I shall adopt a relatively straightforward definition of creative problem solving as the first step in the discussion. For the present, then, creative problem solving involves a person's producing a novel response that solves the problem at hand.

There are two factors which are important in this definition. First, the solution must be novel for the person; creativity involves more than repeating some old solution. Second, novelty in itself is not enough; the solution must indeed solve the problem. If I am trying to solve the problem of getting my car to start, then banging my head against the wall may be a novel response. Other people might think it novel. I might never have done it before, especially in such a situation. However, novel or not, it does not solve my problem, and so it is not creative.

In addition, our interest for the present is with creativity only as far as it concerns the individual. Some believe that for an act to be truly creative, it must not be produced by many individuals; for them, a creative solution must be novel for society as a whole. An example would be the theory of natural selection, produced only by Charles Darwin and Alfred Russell Wallace. For purposes of this discussion, however, any solution which is novel for an individual, regardless of how many other individuals arrive at the same solution, is creative.

Although the discussion begins with an analysis of several seemingly artificial problem solving situations, I hope ultimately to show that similar processes are involved in creative work in science and the arts. The view that creative work in science involves problem solving is straightforward, since in most situations scientists are faced with the problem of devising a theory that explains some phenomenon. Even though creative thought in science works on a much broader scale than the examples discussed in this chapter, the processes are the same, as I show in Chapter 6. I also show in Chapter 7 how creative artists—painters, sculptors, poets, and novelists—can be seen as trying to solve problems. For example, we might think of a painter as trying to solve the problem of expressing in a painting some feelings about his or her life. In addition, the painter may also be trying to produce a painting that will move others emotionally; this can be seen as an attempt to solve another problem. Thus, the present discussion begins with problem solving on the assumption that the conclusions drawn will have broader relevance.

Using an Object in a Novel Way

A recent experience of mine resulted in a creative solution to a relatively simple real-life problem. Although not particularly impressive when compared to the examples of creative problem solving already cited, it did contain the germs of several important ideas concerning the processes underlying creative thinking. The following informal analysis, therefore, will be used as a basis for what is to come.

As I was driving, the car's power brakes failed and I had to press hard on the pedal to stop. I opened the hood and noticed that a section of the master brake cylinder was gleaming white, while everything else was coated with grime. There was a hissing noise coming from the clean part, which was a tube, and when I put my hand there, the hiss stopped and my hand was held in place by suction. With my hand held like this, the brake pedal responded normally. So here was the problem: how to re-cover the tube?

Re-covering the end of the tube was not a particularly difficult problem to solve—cut out a cardboard circle and tape it in place until a permanent repair could be made. Though this solution is not especially impressive, since it involved the relatively direct application of my knowledge to the new situation, it is creative because I had never used cardboard in that way before. Something else happened, however, that made things a bit more interesting.

One problem with the cardboard solution was that the pressure in the tube might be strong enough to collapse the cardboard circle. A metal circle would work better, I thought, and I began thinking about how to fashion one that was about an inch in diameter. As I was mulling this new problem over, I had to stop to pay a toll. As I pulled a quarter from my pocket, I realized that it would solve the problem nicely: it was strong and just about the right size. The quarter turned out to be a good solution and was significantly better than cutting a circle out of cardboard or even metal. This is an example of a creative solution to a problem, involving the use of an ordinary object in a radically novel way.

Assuming that my recollection of this minor creative act is correct, several points should be emphasized. First, the processes involved seem to be relatively straightforward. I was thinking about the problem, but had to leave it briefly to pay the toll. As I found the quarter and took it from my pocket, its shape and feel reminded me of the object I was just thinking about. One of the claims made about the creativity is that to make novel use of an object involves thinking that differs from ordinary conscious thinking. This was not true in the present case: the novel use of a quarter evolved through a straightforward series of conscious steps.

Second, a quarter alone could not have effectively reminded me of the problem if I had not thought about the problem first. I first had to find potential difficulties with the cardboard circle solution and think about the specific aspects the solution called for. If I had thought the cardboard circle would work, I simply would have forgotten the incident and never found an object in the environment that recalled the problem to me.

Finally, it may be true that if I had not just recently thought about my problem, then I might not have seen the quarter as a potential solution. Because the quarter reminded me of the object I needed, the problem was easily recallable. This happens when the problem has just been thought about, has been thought about relatively recently, or has been thought about a great deal in the past. Such recall happens all the time in ordinary situations. If I have something on my mind, I think about other things and attend to objects and events in the environment that are related to it. No additional thought processes are needed when this happens: the problem is on my mind, and things will be related to it. David Perkins, a psychologist who has done extensive research in creativity, presents additional evidence to support this view.

The processes involved in solving my brake-cylinder problem will become relevant when other examples of creative problem solving are discussed later. In these cases rather obvious solutions are also problematic and an object in the environment is made to serve. These same thought processes may be involved in many important acts of scientific creativity; in fact, the literature is full of examples of creative discoveries that seem to be similar to my "discovery" of the quarter. If no unusual processes are needed to explain my novel use of a quarter, then perhaps none are needed to explain the creative solutions produced by scientists.

Creativity in a Simple Laboratory Problem

There are a number of problems studied experimentally by psychologists and their sometimes creative solutions provide further information about how an individual produces a novel solution to a problem. Though these problems are not particularly profound, there are some potentially far-reaching conclusions to be drawn from them. The first problem to be discussed is sometimes solved by using a common object in a novel way.

Consider the situation presented in Figure 1.1. A person is given a candle, a book of matches, and a box of tacks and is instructed to attach the candle to a wooden door, so that there will be light for reading. The candle must burn properly. Using only the objects in the picture, how can the candle be attached to the door? Karl Duncker's "candle problem" has been studied by psychologists for almost 50 years. Most people have lit and manipulated candles but have not tried to attach one to a door. Solving the problem, therefore, requires creative thinking.

Most individuals who attack this problem initially produce one of two general types of solutions. They either try to tack the candle to the door or glue it with melted wax. Because most people have never tacked or glued a candle to a door, there is true creativity involved in proposing these solutions. Furthermore, these solutions can be made to work, so they do solve the problem.

One other, less frequent, type of solution involves tacking the empty tack box to the door and using it as a holder for the candle. This box solution also solves the problem, and does so in a very elegant way. The candle is held up securely, no wax drips, and damage to the wall is minimal. The question of interest then becomes how this solution comes about. What factors determine whether or not a person will use the box as a candle holder?

Verbal Protocols.   One way to begin to answer this question is to ask subjects to verbalize everything they think of as they work on the problem, even seemingly trivial or irrelevant thoughts. Although it is impossible to verbalize everything that occurs while tryng to solve even a simple problem like this, it is possible to produce a more or less continuous stream of talking while one works on it. Psychologists have used this stream of talking, or *verbal protocol,* to study problem solving in many situations, from playing chess to writing poetry. It is important to emphasize that the person is not asked to describe the "workings of their mind," that is, to describe their thought process. They are simply asked to verbalize their thoughts as they work on the problem. It seems that people cannot

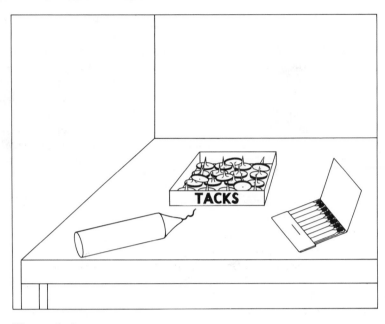

Figure 1.1
The candle problem.

describe very much about the process involved in thinking, though it is possible to think aloud without much difficulty.

The distinction between thinking aloud and describing the thought processes is made in the following hypothetical protocol. For the sake of discussion, let us say that if I had been thinking aloud as I worked on my problem with the brake cylinder, I would have sounded something like this:

> I guess I could cut a piece of cardboard to fit over that hole, and it could be taped—but I'll bet it would collapse. Maybe a circle of metal would work, but can I cut metal?

This is a stream-of-consciousness verbalization, in which relevant thoughts are verbalized. Since I just made it up, it is neater than potocols usually are, but it provides an approximation to a real protocol. Now, consider the *processes* involved in the hypothetical episode presented above. One process might be *remembering* about uses of cardboard; another might be *estimating* how well the cardboard would work, and so on. Given this brief description of but two of the many processes involved in solving a problem, one can see why it is impossible to report much about them. Because many processes occur at nearly the same time, reporting on them is very difficult. Experimental evidence shows that thinking aloud does not greatly change the way a person attacks a problem, so the verbal protocols supply helpful data on the processes ordinarily involved in problem solving.

If one examines the verbal protocols of the few people who produce the box solution to the candle problem, and compares them to the protocols of the majority who do not produce that solution, several interesting conclusions emerge. First, those who ultimately produce the box solution do not begin with it; they, like the others, begin by thinking about tacking or gluing the candle. One difference between the box-users and the others, however, is that the box-users decide that tacking or gluing the candle will not work; once they decide this, they think of using the box. Several excerpts from protocols of subjects working on the candle problem follow; in each case, the person was only *mentally* working on the problem and not physically manipulating the objects involved.

> *Subject 1.* "Candle has to burn straight, so if I took a nail and put it through the candle ... (ten sec) ... if I took several nails and made a row and set the candle on that. If I took the nails out of the box, nailed the box to the wall ..."
>
> *Suject 2.* "Put a nail into the candle so it supports the candle, so as the candle burns it won't fall. But the nail won't go through the candle, so put some nails around the side of the candle to hold it. Use the box ..."
>
> *Subject 3.* "Drive a nail through the candle—a long nail. One problem—a long nail might split the candle. Therefore use a thin nail. You might be able to put up some nails next to each other and burn the candle on them. Or put nails into the wall along the sides of the candle ... There don't seem to be enough nails large enough so you could ... Another way, take the box, etc."

When we examine these protocols, we see that the box-users first thought of attaching the candle directly to the wall with nails, then felt that such a solution would not work. They then considered variations on these "attaching" solutions that involved "platforms" of nails, and then the box was incorporated in one of these solutions. This pattern was found in all the subjects who produced the box solution in the experiment: they first tried a direct attaching solution, realized the difficulties with it, and then tried to remedy those difficulties. In this way, the person's knowledge becomes especially important, because he or she has to think about what is going to happen, rather than simply observing what happens as a solution is attempted. Once it is decided that some sort of platform is needed for the candle, in order to remedy the difficulties, the box is noticed because it can serve as a platform.

Other evidence, in addition to analysis of protocols, supports the idea that the solution evolves out of attempts to remedy inadequacies in earlier solutions. Box solutions, for example, take longer to produce than attaching solutions, as would be expected if box solutions result from modifications of attaching solutions. Also, if an attaching solution is made less likely, by giving subjects additional criteria to meet (i.e., wax cannot drip on the floor), or by making the tacks too small to go through the candle, then the box is used more frequently. These results are also consistent with the notion that attaching solutions are universally considered first (since that is what the problem calls for), because the results indicate that use of the box depends on inadequacies in attaching solutions. The more inadequate that attaching solutions are made, the more likely the box will be used.

From this brief analysis of creative problem solving we can tentatively draw several conclusions about the factors involved in producing a novel solution for this problem. First, the creative solution evolves out of the initial attempts to solve the problem. Furthermore, the protocols indicate that all subjects start at basically the same place, and those who ultimately produce the box solution have no unique insight initially.

This leads to an interesting reanalysis of "creative leaps," at least in the candle problem. If one examines only the initial problem situation and the final box solution, it is hard to see where the solution comes from. There is no obvious connection between the "task" and the solution, and the solution apears to come about in a single creative leap. With a verbal protocol, however, one can see the number of intermediate steps involved, and how each is directly based on what preceeded it. Creative products evolve gradually, and to understand the creative process, one must be able to observe these intermediate steps. If one just looks at the problem and the creative solution, the whole process seems very mysterious.

A second conclusion about this process is that the evolution of the novel solution depends in several ways on the problem solver's knowledge. The box solution first depends on difficulties with other solutions, and these depend on what the person knows about the objects in question. Will the nails split the candle, is the wax strong enough to hold the candle up, or is the box strong enough to support the candle? Once a difficulty occurs in a tentative solution, the person's knowledge again becomes important in overcoming it. The whole problem-solving cycle begins again, with the difficulty in the solution the new problem to be solved. If the difficulty in the tentative solution is overcome, and no other difficuties arise, the whole problem may be solved.

√ Changing Direction on a Problem

If novel solutions evolve in response to specific pieces of information a person acquires as he or she works on a problem, then it should be possible to specify those pieces of information in a given problem. Providing these pieces of information should make solving the problem relatively easy. Evidence to support this claim comes from a study of the following problem.

> *The Charlie Problem.* Dan comes home one night after work, as usual.
> He opens the door and steps into the living room. On the floor he sees
> Charlie lying dead. There is water on the floor, as well as some pieces
> of glass. Tom is also in the room. Dan takes one quick glance at the
> scene and immediately knows what happened. How did Charlie die?

Subjects must determine how Charlie died by asking yes or no questions of the experimenter. The questions and answers are used to determine what information a person has about the problem at any given time. One can then relate the proposed solutions to the information that has been acquired up to that time.

The solution which we were looking for is that Dan's pet fish, Charlie, was swimming in a glass fish bowl and Dan's pet cat, Tom, knocked it to the floor and broke it, causing Charlie to die of lack of oxygen. Discovering this solution usually takes almost an hour. Initially, nearly everyone thinks Charlie and Tom are human and that a drinking glass that once held water has been broken. In order to solve this problem a "transition in thought" must take place in which the initial way of viewing things is set aside and a new analysis of the situation adopted. The question of interest is what factors, if any, produce these transitions in thought. That is, what pieces of information must be acquired before people will change their way of viewing the problem?

The initial assumptions, that the characters are human and the glass comes from a drinking glass, lead subjects to examine the various ways in which humans die. For example, one person suggested that Charlie had heart disease, that Tom hid his pills, and that Charlie had a fatal heart attack and dropped the glass of water that he was holding in anticipation of taking his pills. When everything of this sort produces no progress, the problem solvers then ask questions about various aspects of the situation. The negative answer to whether Charlie had any marks on him, for example, rules out many possibilities (he was not shot or stabbed), leads to more questions about the cause of death, and eventually elicits the fact that Charlie died of lack of oxygen. This information alone, however, is not enough to produce the critical transition. Once people determine that Charlie died of lack of oxygen, *and* that the glass came from a fish bowl, they soon deduce that Charlie is a fish. Thus, about half our subjects make the transition from Charlie-is-a-person to Charlie-is-a-fish by acquiring two critical pieces of information: Charlie died of lack of oxygen, and the glass is from a fish bowl.

Some subjects do not go directly from Charlie-is-a-person to Charlie-is-a-fish; they include Charlie-is-*not-human* in the transition and later discover that he is a fish in a second step. For these subjects, other critical pieces of information, usually different for each person, lead them to realize that Charlie is not human. For example, one person asked about Charlie's age and found that though he might be a year old, he was not an infant. This information leads relatively directly to the notion that Charlie is not a person. Other subjects arrive at Charlie-is-not-human in different ways, but in each case some salient pieces of information essentially force them to.

To summarize, it is possible in this experiment to specify what information produces the critical transition. We found that it comes about in either of two ways; critical pieces of information are involved in each, but the cases are different. The Charlie-is-a-fish transition seems to depend on the person's knowing that Charlie died of lack of oxygen and that the glass was a fishbowl. The Charlie-is-not-human transition involves information that is inconsistent with the assumption that Charlie-is-a-person. We attempted to validate the importance of these pieces of information by including them in further tests with other subjects. Specifically, if certain information is crucial in producing the Charlie-is-a-fish transition, providing it should make solving the problem very easy—subjects should directly conclude that Charlie is a fish. If, on the other hand, other specific information results in the transition to Charlie is not human, then providing it should produce just that transition.

Our results support the above hypothesis. In one experiment, for example, the problem was changed to read: "Charlie died of lack of oxygen and the pieces of glass were from a fishbowl. How did Charlie die from lack of oxygen?" With this information, all subjects produced the expected Charlie-is-a-fish transition and solution times were drastically shortened. Thus, it seems that these transitions in thought are the result of the availability of relatively specific pieces of information as the person works through the problem.

The results from the Charlie problem support those from the candle problem. Novel solutions are produced when the information acquired while working on the problem pushes the problem solver in a new direction. Such a switch may seem to occur suddenly as far as the subjective experience of the problem solver is concerned, but actually it occurs in response to specific aspects of the problem. We have all experienced the sudden flash of excitement when we solve a problem that has troubled us for a while. The results from the Charlie problem show that such a flash does not mean the solution comes from out of the blue, but rather that it evolves from earlier attempts. The sudden excitement accompanying the realization that Charlie is a fish may be due to the fact that the person was working for a while on a frustrating problem. The solution *process* might not be any different from that involved in ordinary problem solving, but it *feels* different because the difficult problem has made one sweat.

Conclusions

This way of analyzing creative problem solving was stimulated by my work on laboratory problems. In our experiments, creative solutions evolved out of the subject's conscious work on the problem. The subject typically first tried to apply his or her knowledge, based on past exprience, directly to the problem, but the design of these problems usually caused such direct attempts to fail, forcing the subject to modify the earlier solution to meet the problem's demands. These modifications were fueled by acquisition of additional information. Though the solution might begin with a straightforward (but unsuccessful) application of past experience, it could evolve into something novel and appropriate, that is, a creative solution to a problem.

This line of thinking leads to a view of creativity which emphasizes the incremental nature of the creative response, in contrast to the "traditional" genius view of creativity which holds that extraordinary thought processes bring about great creative or insightful leaps. Several different, although related, sorts of extraordinary thought processes have been postulated. Some theorists emphasize unconscious thought processes, which they assume can make associative connections that are beyond the capacity of ordinary conscious thinking. Other theorists emphasize spontaneous restructuring as the basis for sudden insight into a problem—this occurs when the problem solver breaks out of the bonds of past experience and sees into the problem's structure. This view also has led to an interest in methods that claim to teach people how to break away from past experience and see in this new way. In addition, the traditional view assumes that certain extraordinary individuals possess a quality called "creative genius," a set of psychological characteristics that provide the basis for their creative capacity. Such a capacity is assumed to be necessary in order to explain certain extraordinary accomplishments, such as the development of great scientific theories or the production of great works of art.

In the view outlined earlier, however, creativity is seen as an activity resulting from the ordinary thought processes of ordinary individuals. This view has both negative and positive implications concerning our understanding of creativity. On the negative side, the problem solving examples discussed to this point make it evident that we are all capable of modifying our behavior to deal with the ever-novel situations we face. If so, then all human actions may involve creativity at their core, indicating that neither extraordinary thought processes nor extraordinary individuals are necessary. This view also emphasizes the dependence of creative acts on past experience, and the gradual evolution of a creative response out of past experience. No great leaps of conscious or unconscious insight necessarily occur. Rather creative action is slow and incremental, the familiar way of dealing with a problem gradually evolving into something new. From this one can see that creativity cannot be taught by encouraging people to break away from past experience, because past experience is the basis for the initial approach to a problem (even though it may be incorrect) and the subsequent modification of an incorrect solution. In my view, creative individuals possess no extraordinary characteristics—basically, they do what we are all capable of doing. Because everyone can modify habitual responses to deal with novel situations, no further extraordinary capacities should be needed. Though in a given case the work an individual produces may be extraordinary, extraordinary work is not necessarily the product of extraordinary processes or the result of extraordinary personal characteristics.

Expertise in Problem Solving

Recent research on problem solving in a variety of domains emphasizes the importance of detailed knowledge, or expertise. Interest in the role of expertise in creative problem solving was stimulated by Adriaan de Groot's effort to understand problem solving in complicated situations by studying the skills of chess masters. When de Groot asked his subjects to think aloud as they chose a move, he found that their thought processes were not remarkably different from those of less skillful players. For example, one might expect a chess master to work through many possible moves before deciding on one. De Groot found just the opposite: master players actually consider very few moves at each turn, but these moves are almost always appropriate.

How does the master know which moves to consider? It appears that through years of study and play masters develop a greatly detailed visual memory of chess positions. They use this knowledge to analyze the position before them and it determines which moves are worth considering. This knowledge is again used to determine how these possible moves must be modified to respond to the specific situation at hand, which seldom matches precisely any situation the master has studied before.

Evidence to support the claim that chess expertise depends upon detailed knowledge about chess is found in de Groot's study of chess masters' memories for chess positions. De Groot exposed chess players of varying degrees of skill to a chess position from the middle of a chess game. After a five-second exposure masters could recall the positions of all the pieces perfectly, while players of lesser skill could recall proportionally less. De Groot's findings were replicated and extended by William Chase and Herbert Simon, who attempted to estimate how much information chess masters had to acquire before they were capable of such feats. Chase and Simon's analysis indicated that chess masters acquire approximately 50,000 patterns, with four or five pieces in each pattern. These patterns are used to analyze all positions they face, and thus serve as the basis for both the "understanding" of the game and their ability to make novel moves in the course of a game.

While acquiring 50,000 patterns is no trivial task, it is important to emphasize that it is not of inhuman proportion. If a young person very interested in chess studies and practices it for 10 years, and to reach master level one must apply oneself to this degree, he or she has spent at least 25,000–35,000 hours thinking about chess. If one learns just two patterns an hour, certainly not an inhuman task, one could acquire the knowledge needed, in Chase and Simon's view, to play chess at the highest level. It should also be noted that ordinary individuals use visual knowledge of a similar magnitude when they read. The average reading vocabulary of a college student is over 20,000 words, and most college students are not as interested in studying words as chess masters are in studying chess.

In summary, de Groot's work emphasized the role of detailed knowledge in developing the capacity to solve problems creatively, at least within the domain of chess.

More recent research has examined the role of expertise in problem solving in other domains, including physics, arithmetic, computer programming, and geometry. The results in all these areas support de Groot's analysis: detailed past experience is crucial in determining how efficiently an individual solves a novel problem. Furthermore, developing expertise involves acquiring much knowledge about specific situations, so that one can initially deal with a new situation on the basis of how it resembles situations one has faced before. Of course, since the situation is new, the knowledge cannot be applied directly and without modification to meet its specific needs. These conclusions closely parallel those drawn earlier concerning the importance of specialized knowledge in problem solving.

In an analysis of the role of expertise in problem solving, James Greeno, a leading theorist in the area, draws several conclusions that summarize the point of view of this book. Recent research, he notes, has blurred the distinction between performance based on knowledge and performance based on problem solving. Until recently, according to Greeno, the performance of someone who used knowledge to deal with a situation was not valued as highly as that of someone who used "real problem solving." It was presumed that real problem solving was not based on ("mere") knowledge, but rather involved working out something new on the basis of one's problem solving abilities. As Greeno notes, however, much of the respect "real problem solving" attracted was due to an inability to identify the knowledge underlying the problem solver's performance. With the recent successes in indentifying such knowledge, therefore, all performances are now recognized as being based on knowledge. The question that remains is how directly one's knowledge is applied.

In addition, Greeno's analysis of studies of experts solving problems, as well as those of individuals dealing with more routine situations, leads him to conclude that the same characteristics are present in both performances, by both individuals, in both situations. There is basically no difference, he says, between the performance of the expert solving a complicated novel problem and that of a nonexpert dealing with a relatively trivial situation that might not ordinarily be thought of as requiring problem solving. Thus, it may be possible to learn a great deal about creativity by considering situations that initially seem to demand little creative thinking.

Finally, with regard to creative problem solving in particular, Greeno emphasizes the need for detailed domain-specific knowledge on the part of those who wish to make original contributions in any area. I agree with Greeno's conclusions.

Outline of the Book

The incremental view of creativity presented in this chapter has both positive and negative implications, and these will be explored throughout the rest of the book. The negative implications regarding the genius view of creativity are explored fully in Chapters 2 through 5. Chapters 2 through 4 concern the notion that extraordinary thought processes underlie creative acts. Chapter 2 critically discusses the assertion that great creative achievements come about through unconscious thought processes. Chapter 3 considers the claims that leaps of creative insight do not depend greatly on past experience, and that past experience can interfere with creative thinking. Chapter 4 examines the idea that creative thinking involves an ability to break away from an old way of viewing a problem and use a special thought process called divergent thinking to generate new ideas in response to the problem. Chapter 5 critically reviews the question of whether specific personality characteristics make up "genius."

On a positive side, an incremental view of creativity leads to the expectation that even impressive creative products are rooted firmly in the experience of the creative individual and are developed gradually from his or her past work, and the work of others. Small steps, in this view, rather than great leaps, are the rule. Furthermore, the thought processes involved in great acts of creativity are like those found in more ordinary activities. Chapters 6 and 7 analyze several well-known examples of creative thinking in science and the arts, providing further evidence for the incremental nature of creative thinking. Finally, Chapter 8 presents an expansion of the incremental viewpoint.

2

productive
innovative

THE MYTH OF
THE UNCONSCIOUS

The appearance of a creative idea can sometimes be very mysterious, even to the person who produced it. One may have been working on a problem for a long while without apparent success, when a soluion suddenly appears "out of the blue," in what seems to be a leap of insight. Such experiences have played an important role in the development of theories of creativity that emphasize unconscious thinking. If one cannot report any thought processes leading to the creative idea, then, according to this line of theorizing, unconscious thought processes must have been involved. This chapter is concerned with two variations on the theme that unconscious processes play a crucial role in creative thinking. The discussion begins with several famous subjective reports of creative achievements, which many assume resulted from the action of unconscious thought processes. Two theories of unconscious thinking in creativity are then considered. The first is Henri Poincaré's theory that the sudden appearance of creative ideas is the result of _incubation,_ a period of unconscious thought. The second theory is Arthur Koestler's theory of _bisociation,_ which combines some of Poincaré's ideas with those of Sigmund Freud. He assumes that the appearance of a creative idea depends on the unconscious combining of ideas in such a way that conscious thinking could not be responsible. Discussion of theory leads to an examination of research that has attempted to demonstrate unconscious thinking in laboratory studies of creativity. The chapter concludes by reconsidering the value of subjective reports as data for a theory of creative thinking.

Examples of the Action of Unconscious
Thought Processes

The traditional literature on creatvity consists mainly of reports from creative scientists, artists, and inventors about how they work. Many of these reports are taken as evidence for the role of unconscious processes in creative thought.

Poincaré Much of the current emphasis on the unconscious in creativity can be traced directly to Poincaré, who presented detailed reports of how he carried out his mathematical work, and who also developed a theory of creativity that emphasized unconscious processes.

The critical segment of Poincaré's work involved his attempt to prove that a certain sort of mathematical function, which he called Fuchsian functions, could not exist. (An understanding of Fuchsian functions is not critical to an understanding of Poincaré's thought processes.) Poincaré worked without success for fifteen days trying to prove that Fuchsian functions could not exist; he worked for several hours at a time and attempted to make various kinds of proofs. One night, after an unsuccessful day, he drank black coffee and could not sleep. As he lay awake "[i]deas rose in crowds; I felt them collide until pairs interlocked, so to speak, making a stable combination." After this sleepless night of thinking, Poincaré established that his original idea was incorrect—one example of a Fuchsian function could be proved to exist. Poincaré was obviously conscious when these ideas arose, but he felt the thinking was of an extraordinary sort since it occurred during sleeplessness brought on by the coffee. Because he felt himself to be an inactive participant, he concluded that he was essentially observing the workings of his own unconscious.

Poincaré then went on vacation and made another discovery. While boarding an omnibus he suddenly realized that the Fuchsian functions were identical to a set of functions already existing in mathematics, the transformations of non-Euclidean geometry.

> The incidents of travel made me forget my mathematical work. Having reached Coutances, we entered an omnibus to go some place or other. At the moment when I put my foot on the step, the idea came to me, without anything in my former thoughts seeming to have paved the way for it . . . I did not verify the idea; I should not have had time, as, upon taking my seat in the omnibus, I went on with a conversation already commenced, but I felt a perfect certainty. On my return to Caen, for conscience' sake, I verified the result at my leisure.

There are several important points about Poincaré's report of this incident. First, he was not thinking of mathematics while on the excursion. Second, when the idea appeared, none of his previous thoughts seemed to lead up to it. That is, he was engaged in a conversation about something else when the flash of insight occurred. Third, Poincaré felt certain the idea was correct without having to verify it. These factors led him and others to believe that unconscious processes are important in creativity. The leap that Poincaré made must have been brought about by unconscious work, so the argument goes. That is, although he was not *consciously* working on the problem while on vacation, he was *unconsciously* working on it.

Poincaré could not verify the insight at that time, but did so when he returned from his trip. Several hours of conscious work then demonstrated that his insight had indeed been correct. A similar phenomenon occurred to him later in the same investigation. He was stumped while working on a problem, went to do something else, and again the solution to his problem suddenly came to him. without his working on it.

These examples of Poincaré's are often cited as phenomena demonstrating the importance of unconscious processes in creative problem solving. This interpretation was proposed by Poincaré himself, who said that the sudden appearance of the solution, or the sudden "illumination," was "a manifest sign of long, unconscious prior work. The role of this unconscious work in mathematical invention appears to me incontestable." Although in this case Poincaré was discussing mathematical invention, others have argued that similar processes are at work in all creative thinking.

Mozart   Another often-cited example of unconscious processes is Mozart's report of how he composed.

> When I feel well and in a good humor, or when I am taking a drive or walking after a good meal, or in the night when I cannot sleep, thoughts crowd into my mind as easily as you could wish. Whence and how do they come? I do not know and I have nothing to do with it. Those which please me, I keep in my head and hum them; at least others have told me that I do so. Once I have my theme, another melody comes, linking itself to the first one, in accordance to the needs of the composition as a whole.

As in the example from Poincaré, Mozart reported that the music came into consciousness without any particular work on his part. The creation of a melody was done before Mozart became conscious of anything. He did not have to edit anything; the melodies were not reworked or changed, he simply kept the ones he liked in his head and hummed them. Salieri may have believed these melodies were the voice of God, but the modern view assumes that the completed melodies were worked out in Mozart's unconscious mind.

Mozart's methods were perhaps even more striking than Poincaré's. Poincaré began with fifteen days of hard work before going on vacation, but Mozart reported that his melodies came to him without any prior work at all. He did not, for example, try to compose a symphony, give up in disgust, and then have a lovely melody suddenly occur to him. Mozart's melodies apparently came to him without any conscious preparation on his part at all. When pondering where Mozart's melodies might have come from, a plausible answer is that they came from the unconscious.

Coleridge   A final example involves Samuel Taylor Coleridge's creation of the poem *Kubla Khan*. According to Coleridge's report he had been in ill health and living alone in a secluded farmhouse. One afternoon, because of "a slight indisposition," he took a dose of "an anodyne" (two grams of opium) "which had been prescribed." (Coleridge's probable addiction to opium at the time *Kubla Kahn* was written has contributed much to the mystery and interest surrounding the poem's creation.) After taking the drug, he fell asleep in a chair while reading a passage from "Purchas's Pilgrimage," a large book of tales of exotic places, and very well known at the time. The passage read: "Here the Khan Kubla commended a palace to be built, and a stately garden thereunto. And thus ten miles of fertile ground were enclosed with a wall." Coleridge reports that during this sleep a poem came to him. (In the following passage, Coleridge calls himself "the Author.")

> The Author continued for about three hours in a profound sleep, at least of the external senses, during which time he had the most vivid confidence that he could not have composed less than from two to three hundred lines; if that indeed can be called composition in which all the images rose up before him as *things,* with a parallel production of the concurrent expressions, without any sensation or consciousness of effort. On awakening he appeared to himself to have a distinct recollection of the whole, and taking his pen, ink, and paper, instantly and eagerly wrote down the lines that are here preserved. At this moment he was unfortunately called out by a person on business from Porlock, and detained by him above an hour, and on his return to his room, found, to his no small surprise and mortification, that though he still retained some vague and dim recollection of the general purport of the vision, yet, with the exception of some eight or ten lines and images, all the rest had passed away like the images on the surface of a stream into which a stone has been cast, but alas! without the after restoration of the latter!

This is yet another report in which a final product, in this case a poem, appears effortlessly to the creator, without any prior work on the creator's part. As with Mozart's report of his composing melodies, Coleridge states that what happened could not really be called composing, because the lines of the poem simply occurred to him "without any sensation or consciousness of effort," as an accompaniment to the visual images he was experiencing. No prior preparation was reported by Coleridge, save that he had been reading related material when he fell asleep.

Coleridge's report is also important because it is an example of creativity occurring during an altered state of consciousness. There are many examples of creative acts occurring during a state other than ordinary consciousness. Poincaré's report of his sleepless night brought on by black coffee is such example, as are reports of solving problems during dreams, or while under the influence of alcohol. Reports of creative acts occurring during such states support the commonly held notion that altered states allow unconscious processes to operate freely.

Jumping the Gap

Though but a small sample, these three reports make clear the various phenomena that are thought to occur when creative thought is going on. In each there is a relatively large gap between where the person stopped work and the final product. Mozart, for example, reported that he produced his music without any prior composing, thus, the gap here lies between Mozart not thinking about music and the sudden occurrence of melodies to him. Furthermore, Mozart produced complete musical pieces without any tentative steps, false starts, revision, or editing. His humming of melodies that pleased him could be considered editing of a sort, but even those melodies that displeased him occurred in complete form, and were simply rejected completely. Other complete melodies then came to replace them. This is not what one normally considers editing, with deleting and reworking of musical phrases note by note, and so on. The intricate work involved in producing the symphonic pieces Mozart talked about must have been carried out in *some* way. Again, it seems reasonable to argue that this work was done in his unconscious, before he ever became aware of anything.

In a similar manner, Coleridge produced a complete poem without any tentative steps. Again, there were no false starts, correcting, or editing. Though "Purchas's Pilgrimage" may have been a stimulus, the gap between it and what Coleridge produced is large enough to warrant some intervening steps. Once again, many conclude that those steps occurred in his unconscious.

To summarize, postulating unconscious thought seems reasonable when the thought process "jumps a gap," and no external aid to help the thinker across the gap is apparent. If a series of steps are involved in jumping this gap, then they must have been carried out unconsciously. If the thinking involves only a small step, then postulating the existence of complicated unconscious processes is unnecessary.

After-the-Fact Reports

Each of the three examples just considered are subjective reports made by creators after the event occurred. For Poincaré and Coleridge especially, the reports were made relatively long afterwards. There are a number of reasons why one must be wary of such reports. First is the potential problem of the author's memory. Obviously, if an incident is reported long after it occurs, there is a chance the person will have forgotten some significant aspects of the event in the interim. Furthermore, there is the risk of *distorted* recall of an earlier event. That is, not only might parts of the event be forgotten, but new information might be recalled that was never part of the original event at all. Also, it is seldom possible to tell if the subjective report is accurate. How would one know whether or not Poincaré actually had that insight while stepping on the omnibus? How do we know there was no cue in the environment to stimulate his thought that he later forgot? Since all we have in this case is Poincaré's report, we can go no further.

Because we cannot verify most of these reports, we must be cautious in dealing with creators' reports of what they do. For the time being, however, I will assume that the reports of Poincaré, Mozart, and Coleridge are reasonably accurate. I do this to show that there is still not a very strong case to be made for the role of unconscious processes in creative thinking.

The Four Stages in Creative Problem Solving

Based on reports such as those discussed earlier, Graham Wallas proposes there are four stages in all creative acts. Poincaré's creative insight on the omnibus is a concrete example of these stages. The first stage, *preparation,* involves a long period of intense conscious work, without success. Poincaré, for example, worked for fifteen days. After this period of preparation, the problem is often put aside, and not thought about consciously. During this time, according to Wallas and others, *incubation* occurs. Poincaré's going on vacation is an example of this second stage. The problem is not consciously thought about, but work continues unconsciously. If the incubation stage is successful, then in the next stage the person experiences a sudden *illumination,* a sudden insight into the solution of the problem. This happened to Poincaré when he entered the omnibus. As in Poincaré's case, the illumination is often accompanied by a feeling of certainty that the solution is correct.

The illummination stage usually produces only a glimmer of the solution, however, with *verification,* Wallas's final stage, being worked out later. Poincaré said he verified "for conscience' sake" the accuracy of his insight. He was sure he was right when the illumination first occurred, and only verified it because of his obligation to others. Hence his mention of his conscience. Poincaré reported that verification of the correctness of the illumination took several hours after returning from the geological expedition.

Of Wallas's four stages, the present discussion is most directly concerned with incubation, because it is the stage in which unconscious thinking is assumed to occur.

A Glimpse into the Unconscious

According to Poincaré and others, such as Jacques Hadamard, a mathematician interested in creative thinking in mathematics, Poincaré's experience of ideas rising in crowds, and colliding together until some combined into pairs is an example of the unconscious at work.

Hadamard's theorizing comes directly from Poincaré's own views: they both claim that invention and discovery involve the combining of ideas. Hadamard makes special note of the fact that the Latin word for thinking, *cogitatio,* comes from *cum* and *agitare* which mean to shake together. Since we possess many thoughts, a tremendous number of possible idea combinations exist when we try to solve a problem. Most of these combinations are of no interest to us, however —but those we do become aware of seem to be potentially fruitful, as, for example, Poincaré's thought that the Fuchsian functions were equivalent to the transformations of non-Euclidean geometry. According to the view developed by Poincaré, and carried forth by others, the unconscious conducts the mental act of combining thoughts, judges the potential value of each combination, and "informs" the conscious of those that are valuable.

One problem that arises when considering the unconscious work involved in combining ideas is the enormous number of possible combinations. Poincaré himself did not believe the unconscious could work through such a large number. He concluded, therefore, that an initial stage of conscious work, Wallas's stage of preparation, was important in determining which combinations of thoughts the unconscious had to consider. In this stage certain thoughts are consciously considered as possible solutions to the problem. If none are successful, then during the second stage, incubation, a person considers thought combinations that begin with the thoughts "activated" during preparation. In any unconscious combination of thoughts, one or both will have been initially considered during preparation. According to Poincaré's point of view, therefore, the unconscious must deal with only a limited number of combinations and the combinations so considered will be relevant to the problem. These combinations then serve as the basis for incubation. If a combination of ideas is positively evaluated, the person will suddenly become conscious of it and experience a sudden illumination.

One may ask, however, what the basis is for a person's unconscious evaluation of any given combination of thoughts. That is, once the unconscious begins combining these thoughts, how does someone suddenly realize that one combination is a potential solution? Poincaré and others believe that such a judgment is an *esthetic* one, based on an individual's sense of beauty. Thought combinations with potential usefulness appeal to the esthetic sensibility of the unconscious because they are particularly "beautiful" or "elegant." Poincaré emphasizes the fact that scientists and mathematicians often talk about the beauty of a theory or the ugliness of a proof, and this, he feels, demonstrates a similarity between scientists and artists—scientists also rely on their intuition of beauty when they make leaps of the imagination. This is why Poincaré felt sure his illumination concerning the Fuchsian functions and non-Euclidean geometry was correct—it was accompanied by a sense of certainty that was based on an esthetic judgment made by his unconscious.

To summarize Poincaré's theory, discovery and invention (problem solving) involve combinations of thoughts. When we work on problems, however, we are consciously aware of only a small number of combinations that are potentially relevant. Many valueless combinations are tested and rejected by the unconscious, but the combinations we become aware of are those that appeal to our esthetic sense, or sense of beauty. Thus, creative problem solving in science or mathematics is similar to artistic creativity.

Koestler's Bisociation Theory

Though the unconscious is important in Poincaré's theory of creativity, its role is not very complicated. All it does during incubation is combine ideas that were "activated" during earlier conscious work on the problem. Arthur Koestler's theory of creativity combines Poincaré's view with a more intricate analysis of the unconscious that is based on Freud's theory.

Koestler's basic assumption about problem solving is the same as Poincaré's: solving a problem involves combining thoughts, and creative problem solving involves joining novel combinations. Koestler also notes that the derivation of the Greek word for thinking, "cogito," originally meant "to shake together." To use Koestler's own metaphor: the history of science can be seen as many marriages of ideas previously thought to be strangers or incompatible, and the matchmaker in these marriages is the unconscious. For example, the phases of the moon and the rising and falling of the ocean tides were both observed and recorded in ancient times, but the potential relationship between the two phenomena went undiscovered until the Roman naturalist Pliny proposed that the moon controlled the tides. Thus, two ideas which had been strangers were married. Furthermore, as often happens with a creative combination of ideas, many people felt that Pliny's connection was incorrect. Even the creative scientist Galileo rejected Pliny's proposal.

Gutenberg's invention of the printing press is another example of such a marriage. Supposedly, Gutenberg's work on how to print letters on paper began by considering the seals used to press letters into wax. He could not invision how a large number of seals could be pressed down on a paper at the same time, thereby printing an entire page. One day at a wine festival, when he had some wine himself, he examined a wine press (essentially a flat surface by which a very strong uniform force is applied over a large area) and realized that a similar device could be used to press many letter seals onto paper. And so the printing press was born. Again, we have the marriage of two unrelated ideas, the letter seal and the wine press.

Koestler proposed the term *bisociation* for the process whereby previously unrelated ideas are brought together and combined. Bisociation is contrasted with association by Koestler, since association refers to previously established connections among ideas, while bisociation involves making connections where none existed before. Every creative act involves such a connection, or bisociation, according to Koestler, and he interprets many examples from the history of science in this way, such as the invention of the printing press.

According to Koestler's theory, ideas exist in interrelated sets, or matrices. In normal conscious, associative, thinking, one idea leads to another idea within the same matrix. In situations demanding creative thinking, however, the thinker must move from one matrix to another. In his discovery of the printing press, for example, Gutenberg began by thinking about pressing letters on paper. At the critical point, however, he moved into the matrix of the wine press. The combination of these two ideas, or their bisociation, led to the creative discovery. According to Koestler, bisociation only occurs when the person has been thoroughly immersed in the problem for a long time. Only after intense mental work will the problem "ripen" sufficiently to enable the bisociative connection between two matrices to be made. The reason the wine press became "bisociated" to the letter press, for example, is because Gutenberg apparently spent much time in deep concentration on the problem and was ready to respond to the chance occurrence of the wine press and see its relevance to his problem.

In considering the mechanism by which bisociation occurs, Koestler, like Poincaré, emphasizes the unconscious, though his view of it is more complicated since he accepts Freud's theory.

The Freudian Unconscious   In his theorizing about unconscious processes in behavior, Freud distinguished between two basic kinds of thought: primary-process thought and secondary-process thought. Secondary-process thought falls under the control of the ego. It is conscious, rational, follows the rules of logic, and is tied to experience. Thus, the thought of food may lead to the thought of one's kitchen because these two phenomena are related in experience. Primary-process thought, on the other hand, is unconscious and controlled by the id. The only controlling factor in primary-process thought is the fulfillment of wishes and needs; in bringing this about the ordinary laws of logic and causality are circumvented. Primary-process thought is thus "freer" than secondary-process thinking, although it does follow its own logic. Therefore, two thoughts that would ordinarily seem unrelated (to the conscious thinker, at least) can be joined in primary-process thinking. In dreams, for example, which according to Freud depend on primary-process thought, one person can symbolize both a beloved and a hated person. This combining of opposites into one symbol violates the ordinary logic of secondary-process thought, but is perfectly acceptable within the logic of the primary-process.

Koestler emphasizes the importance of dreams in his discussion of creative thinking. During dreaming all the conscious controls on thought are relaxed and one is free of the habitual associative connections that usually work to limit thought to a single matrix. Thus, according to Koestler, "while dreaming we constantly bisociate in a passive way." That is, dreaming involves bisociation, but in a passive way, because people seldom work on a problem when dreaming. Unconscious thought can serve to bring about novel combinations of ideas because it is less rigid and specialized than conscious thought. Thought that occurs during dreams, daydreams or in the minds of children is not tied to the rigid laws of conscious thought that adults use. Koestler believes that everything is possible in dreams and other related states, that any thought can be connected to any other thought then. Scientists must rely on this sort of thinking, just as poets do, because they try to create analogies between seemingly nonanalogous things. Pliny's creation of the analogy between the phases of the moon and the tides is such an example. Furthermore, the mental act of discovery, or the creation of a new analogy, is not based on facts—one does not know that the analogy will be useful until after it is proposed. The initial proposal of the analogy, therefore, is a leap into the unknown. Koestler believes this leap is based on emotional factors, that the analogy first strikes a chord in the unconscious and then we become aware of having thought of it. This is very similar to Poincaré's theory of esthetic judgments in the evaluation of ideas.

To summarize, the connection between Koestler's view and that of Poincaré seems clear. Both believe that creativity involves novel combinations of ideas, and that these combinations are tested by the unconscious. Potentially useful combinations are presented to the conscious mind in the form of illuminations, where they are considered further. Now that the hypothesized role of the unconscious has been specified in some detail, I will examine research designed to test the idea that breaking away from a problem is helpful because it promotes incubation, that is, the unconscious combining of ideas.

Unconscious Incubation versus Automatic Processing   A recent surge of interest in cognitive psychology has focused on the possible role of unconscious processes in psychological functioning. Research indicates that it may be possible to analyze the meaning of a stimulus without being aware of its identity, which could be called unconscious or subliminal perception. Psychologists are also interested in how humans perform well-learned skills, such as walking or driving a car, without consciously attending to every minute element they entail. In fact, it seems that these skills are performed better when they are not attended to in detail. If one tries to be aware of every movement made while walking, one is likely to fall on one's face.

I mention this recent work to emphasize the difference between these unconscious or automatic processes and the unconscious incubation postulated by Poincaré, Wallas, and other theorists. When Poincaré refers to unconscious thinking in problem solving, he does not mean the automatic running off of some highly practiced skill, he is talking about new combinations of ideas that are brought about in the unconscious, which is something very different. Though in this chapter I do not claim that humans never process information automatically, I would like to raise the possibility that they do not produce novel solutions to problems through unconscious combination and evaluation of ideas, that is, through unconscious incubation.

Testing for Incubation

Before turning to studies interested in the occurrence of incubation, it is necessary to clarify how the term is to be used. I use the term incubation to refer to a period of time in which a person is not consciously thinking about a problem, but is supposedly unconsciously working on it. This is how Poincaré, Wallas, and others use the term. The existance of an incubation period (that is, of unconscious work) is proved by the sudden illumination a person experiences which would involve several steps if it occurred in conscious thought and which is not stimulated by the environment. The term incubation is used sometimes to refer simply to time spent away from the problem, however, whether or not it ends with an illumination. Based on this latter view, incubation occurs if the person performs better with a break than without it. Poincaré does not see the term in this sense—by his definition, the time away from the problem must end with a sudden illumination that produces a method for solving the problem that is new and unrelated to what preceded it. In my discussion of incubation, I refer to Poincaré's definition.

Several distinctions must be made to make things clear. For instance, does breaking away from the problem help one to solve it? Obviously, if taking a break does not even help, then incubation has not occurred, and all further questions are irrelevant. The fact that such breaks do help people solve problems, however, does not mean that incubation occurs, or that unconscious thought processes take place. For example, Robert Olton talks about "creative worrying," which refers to brief episodes of mulling over the problem while one does something else during the break. This constitutes conscious work on the problem, not incubation. Even if the person does no work at all on the problem during the break, true incubation has not necessarily occurred. There are several psychological explanations for why breaking away from a problem might help one to solve it that have nothing to do with the idea of incubation. One such explanation is the notion that a break might simply provide a rest that results in better performance afterwards.

In two studies, Catherine Patrick studied creative thinking in artists and poets. In response to her questions most of the artists and poets reported that Wallas's four-stage process (preparation, incubation, illumination, and verification) described their work. They said that an idea for a painting or a poem was not worked on immediately, but was first "carried around" for a period of time. Though this seems at first glance to correspond to incubation, Patrick also found that the idea was thought about occasionally during the incubation period (Olton's creative worrying). There was a chance that the idea was worked on at these times, although it was not "definitely related to a specific goal." Patrick felt that illumination or inspiration had occurred when the artist or poet advanced to the stage of being ready to work. It is important, in my opinion, that the artists and poets reported consciously thinking about the idea from time to time during the "incubation" interval because it raises obvious questions: must we assume that unconscious thought occurred, and could the conscious work done during this period have been enough to move the thought processes forward? These reports from artists and poets, therefore, fail to support the notion of unconscious incubation in creativity.

Patrick also attempted to study the four stages of creativity experimentally. In one study, poets were given a picture of a mountainous landscape and asked to write a poem in response to it. Artists were given a poem as a stimulus for a painting. Although the situation was somewhat artificial, neither group felt hampered by the conditions or had much difficulty producing works of good quality. The typical sequence of production began with general impressions and recalling of relevant memories in response to the stimulus, but no concrete work was done. This was followed by a few lines of poetry or the blocking out of a picture; these products were subsequently revised and elaborated. Such behaviors seem to correspond reasonably well to Wallas's stges of preparation, illumination, and verification. (In this case, verification is *revision*, when an early idea is modified or elaborated.) The stages were not completely separate, however, parts of the various stages overlapped in time. Jan Eindhoven and Edgar Vinacke conducted a similar study with artists and found it was impossible to identify separate stages at all, because of the overlap between preparation, illumination, and verification (critical revision).

Patrick's evidence for incubation, in my view, is not relevant to the present discussion at all, because the poets and artists her experiments did not take a break from the problem. On the whole, her work does not support the hypothesis that unconscious thought processes are important in creative thinking. Her interviews indicate that the poets and artists often consciously thougnt about their work during time away from it. Furthermore, the various stages of creative thought postulated by Wallas are not easily seen in her work or that of Eindhoven and Vinacke.

In an interesting and important series of studies, Olton and his associates tried to replicate the important factors involved in a problem-solving situation such as that described by Poincaré. By observing expert chess players trying to solve a chess problem, they hoped to see "evidence" of incubation. In this situation, the domain was thoroughly familiar, and the problem was the sort that the subjects would ordinarily do on their own, which roughly corresponds to Poincaré's work on a mathematical problem. The chess players were divided into two groups, each had several hours to work on the problem, but one group was given a break while the other worked continuously. The group given the break was asked not to work on the problem during the break in order to give unconscious incubation a chance to work. All things considered, this study makes a good attempt to bring the important aspects of incubation situations into the laboratory, yet it uncovered no evidence for unconscious incubation, much to Olton's surprise. The group given a break performed no better on the whole than the group without a break.

This experiment, and negative findings from several earlier ones, led Olton to question whether incubation actually occurs, despite his belief in its existence. A further setback for the incubation theory is found in Olton's inability to replicate other studies that reported finding evidence of incubation. In conclusion, it seems that incubation is difficult to document in controlled situations.

Several recent experiments have shed additional light on the occurrence of incubation in thinking. J. Don Read and Darryl Bruce studied the recall of hard-to-remember pieces of information, when the act of recalling the information might take days or weeks. This is a very common experience—one tries to remember the name of a grade-school teacher, but the name does not come to mind for several days. Read and Bruce tried to determine how such information is remembered. Subjects were shown pictures of television actors from the 1960s whose names, according to earlier testing, were not immediately recallable by everyone. When a subject was unable to recall the actor's name, he or she was excused for a week and asked to keep a diary of all attempts to recall the name during that time. They also were asked to report the circumstances surrounding the successful recall of any names. Read and Bruce's subjects used many strategies in trying to recall the forgotten names, such as thinking about what the person's voice sounded like, or whom the person was married to in real life, or thinking about another role the actor had played.

Read and Bruce tabulated the number of times subjects reported that the name simply "popped into their head" at a time when they were not actively trying to recall it. They considered such examples of recall to be the result of unconscious incubation. Only about 4 percent of the successful recalls involved "spontaneous" remembering of the name. Furthermore, most of incidents of spontaneous recall were reported by just four of the thirty test subjects; when their input is excluded, the proportion of spontaneous recalls falls to nearly zero. As with Olton's work, it is important to emphasize that Read and Bruce's test conditions provided ample opportunity for unconscious incubation to occur in recall, if it were going to. The results gathered by both research teams make it difficult to believe that unconscious processes are widespread in controlled situations. Several other studies also report the either nonexistent or very infrequent incidence of spontaneous recall. Read and Bruce conclude that "the case for the hypothesis of autonomous unconscious work based upon the memory lapse data is practically nonexistent."

Though not directly relevant to the question of unconscious processes in the thinking of Poincaré, Mozart, Coleridge, and the like, these experimental results do raise indirect questions about the accountability of the reports considered at the beginning of the chapter. Given the difficulty of observing incubation in the laboratory, where one has some control over events, how should one evaluate random reports of incubation in which events are not controlled in any way? As I mentioned initially, I wish to question the theory of unconscious incubation in problem solving. Though these laboratory studies raise doubts, someone who truly believed in incubation might argue that they are not relevant, because they show that incubation occurs only to a select few in highly specific situations. That is, it could be argued that what makes Poincaré, Mozart, and Coleridge geniuses is precisely that they experience incubations, while the rest of us do not. This view places heavy emphasis on the subjective reports of creative individuals, making it important to examine those reports more closely.

In the next several sections, I examine in some detail the three subjective reports with which the chapter began. I maintain that such reports are of little value as evidence for a theory of creative thinking. Since such reports are plausible at first glance, it is important for my purposes to show that they must be examined very skeptically indeed.

Mozart's Methods

Both Mozart and Coleridge reported that they produced complete compositions without any preparation. As mentioned earlier, however, there is some question as to whether we should believe these reports. There is strong evidence that Mozart never wrote that letter so frequently quoted and that it is a forgery. Furthermore, Mozart's notebooks contain compositions that were only begun and never completed, or begun, dropped, and then returned to and revised, indicating that things did not always flow as smoothly as the letter implies. Furthermore, Mozart's excellent memory for music might have enabled him to produce completed compositions on paper that had already been more laboriously worked out in his head.

Coleridge, Dreams, and Kubla Khan

Coleridge's report of his opium dream of *Kubla Khan* has interested poetry critics considerably. One of these critics, Elisabeth Schneider, analyzed *Kubla Khan* carefully, and concluded that almost everything Coleridge reported about the poem's creation is probably untrue. According to Schneider, the poem was not created in a dream, it did not suddenly appear in its completed form, and opium probably had little or nothing to do with its creation.

First, another version of the poem was discovered that is slightly different from the final version in ways that suggest it was written earlier. If so, then Coleridge apparently did some editorial work on the poem, indicating that it was not perfect when it "appeared" to him. Also, this other version of the poem was accompanied by an introduction that differed slightly from the introduction reported earlier. Most importantly, Coleridge says that the poem was composed in "a sort of Reverie," which is different than a *dream*. Schneider also notes that Coleridge was notorious for not telling the truth, including when he discussed his work. Thus, in addition to the problems of inaccuracy in subjective reports, there is also the question of their truthfulness. Finally, Schneider also discusses the effects of opium and concludes that it would not induce the "visions" Coleridge reported accompanied the words of the poem.

Schneider also raises an interesting hypothesis as to why Coleridge might have produced such an elaborate fabrication concerning *Kubla Khan's* birth. The poem is not complete, and, according to Schneider, Coleridge might have tried and been unable to complete it, so he was essentially left with an unpublishable fragment. If the fragment is all that remains of a complete poem that appeared in a miraculous dream, however, then it possesses great value. Whether or not one accepts Schneider's speculations concerning Coleridge's motives, her analysis indicates that his report does not support the idea that unconscious processes are important in creativity.

To summarize, under close analysis, some of the subjective reports in the traditional literature turn out to provide no support for the notion of unconscious processes, and neither does controlled laboratory work. Of course, this does not prove that all subjective reports of incubation are untrue, but it does show that relying on them is a mistake.

Solutions without Stimuli?

One remaining aspect of the unconscious thought view is the claim that a solution to a problem can spontaneously spring to mind, without any environmental event or prior conscious thoughts preceding it. An example of such spontaneity is Poincaré's reported insight on the omnibus. He was not talking or thinking about mathematics when it suddenly occurred to him that Fuchsian functions were equivalent to the transformations of non-Euclidean geometry. Since the accuracy of other aspects of the unconscious are doubtful, it is not surprising that reports of solutions to problems occurring spontaneously also are questionable. The first question is raised by the studies of memory retrieval discussed previously. These studies found little or no evidence for spontaneous recall of information.

Furthermore, Norman Maier's study demonstrates that one cannot always accurately report what environmental events influence one's thinking. In Maier's study, subjects were given the task of tying together two strings hanging from the ceiling. The problem is that the strings are positioned so that they cannot both be grasped at once. One way to solve the problem is to swing one string like a pendulum, grasp the other string, and wait until the pendulum string swings close enough to be grasped. Most of Maier's subjects had not thought of the pendulum solution after an hour of work on the problem. They were then given a hint: the experimenter walked past one of the strings and brushed it aside, "accidentally" setting it in pendulum-like motion. This hint was clearly effective because a significant number of the subjects solved the problem soon afterwards.

Once the problem was solved, Maier asked if anything in the environment had helped in finding the solution. About half of those who solved the problem soon after being given the hint were unable to report anything at all about the hint. As far as they were concerned, the solution just "popped" into their heads spontaneously. The implication is reports of spontenous solutions to problems may be completely inaccurate. One can be influenced by a stimulus without being able to report it. A stimulus may be present, the person may be aware of it, it may even have a direct influence on their producing the solution to a problem, but the person may forget all about it. In the excitement of finally solving a stubborn problem, it is understandable that one forgets some of the specific events involved. This may even occur in reports that are made immediately after the solution is found, as in the Maier study. Given the relatively long time that elapsed in Poincaré's case, it is not at all implausible that he forgot some important stimuli that influenced his "spontaneous" realization.

Something of this sort happened to me recently. I was thinking about a problem and made a small "leap of insight" that seemed to be based on an environment cue. I made a mental note to include a discussion of the event here but did not immediately write down the details of the incident, and when I later returned to it could remember nothing more than that I had been assisted by an environmental event when solving a problem. I could remember neither the problem nor the event. As this episode indicates, even if one wants very much to remember all the facts involved in solving a problem, doing so may be very difficult. A person's report of the spontaneous occurrence of an idea, therefore, may be the result of their having forgotten various aspects of the situation. This is most prone to happen when, like Poincaré, the person is not at the time particularly interested in recalling the event as completely as possible. This analysis leaves one final question concerning Poincaré's report: What did he forget?

Poincaré's Creative Worrying   Consider the following situation. A person works on a difficult problem, spending several hours a day in concentrated effort. The person is renown in his or her field and believes that the problem in question is important. Therefore, the problem is central in the person's daily activities. The person works on the problem for more than two weeks, and then goes on vacation. Would this person simply forget about the problem while on vacation? This seems unlikely. It is more reasonable to suppose that such a person would "creatively worry" about the problem while on the trip.

Obviously, the description just given is meant to correspond to Poincaré, who worked for more than two weeks without success before going on a geological expedition. Though there is no direct evidence to support the notion that Poincaré consciously worked on his problem while on vacation, his own report reveals something about his work habits. He worked for more than two weeks without success. Each day, he sat at his desk for several hours, trying to devise a proof. If nothing else, Poincaré was extremely persistent. Anyone who has worked unsuccessfully at a problem knows how hard it is and yet Poincaré persevered for 15 days straight before leaving. He did not go on vacation to get away from his work, rather the work was interrupted by a trip that had been planned earlier. Under these circumstances, it is unlikely that such a person would forget his work, especially when the trip itself was conducted by the geology department of his own university. There is an amusing report in the literature concerning J. Teeple, a chemist, who was so wrapped up in his work that one morning he took a bath, and then was halfway through a second one when he realized that it was not his first bath of the morning. If Poincaré's powers of concentration were of the same magnitude, and his own report hints that they were, then it is hard to believe that he simply forgot his work when he went on vacation.

Conclusions Concerning Incubation

There are now several different reasons for skepticism about the role of incubation in creative problem solving. First, the work of Patrick and of Eindhoven and Vinacke do not verify it or any of the stages postulated by Wallas. Second, a number of laboratory studies have produced only very weak evidence for unconscious processes in thinking, even though they were designed to give adequate opportunity for incubation to occur. The results of these laboratory studies coincide with Patrick's, since Patrick's artists and poets reported that they returned to their original ideas and revised them as they formulated their work, indicating that much of what went on involved conscious processes. Third, some of the reports that seem to provide the strongest evidence for unconscious processes are simply untrue. Thus, contrary to popular opinion, the traditional and modern literature on creativity and problem solving seem in the light of careful analysis to provide little real support for unconscious processes in problem solving.

Alternative Accounts of Incubation

Even if the research considered thus far is wrong, and taking a break is important, there are explanations of why taking a break is helpful which do not include the notion of unconscious thinking. These explanations have existed for a long time, but the unconscious view is so appealing that almost no attention has been paid to the alternatives. Given the doubts raised about unconscious incubation, these other explanations are now worth considering briefly.

A break might be helpful simply because it allows a fatigued person to recuperate. Working on a problem is hard, and working unsuccessfully on a problem is especially hard. It can tire a person and result in less than maximum efficiency of thinking. Taking a break is restorative and increases the person's capacity to think. It is possible, on the other hand, that forgetting is what is needed. A person may be unable to solve a problem because he or she is approaching it in the wrong way. If so, a break might enable them to forget the incorrect approach, thereby making it easier to think of a different, potentially more successful approach.

Again, if one is unsuccessful in solving a problem, it may be because one is attacking it in the wrong way. A method of attacking a problem is called a "set," so one could say that the difficulty is due to the person's having the wrong set for the problem. Taking a break may help the person adopt a new set, and thereby solve the problem. One reason a person might return to the problem with a new set is that some experience during the break affected how he or she wished to approach the problem. For example, I might be trying to solve the Charlie problem by considering human deaths. During the break I walk past a pet store. When I return to the problem, I might be more likely to think of Charlie as a fish.

Finally, it is worth emphasizing again that taking a break might help because during it the person mulls over the problem consciously. This is Olton's "creative worrying" view, and it maintains that a break is not really a break at all, since the person continues to work. Based on this view, one does not have to explain how a break is helpful, because people who "creatively worry" do not really take breaks. This explanation is potentially relevant to Poincaré's reported insight on the omnibus.

In sum, even if taking a break is an important phenomenon in creative problem solving, it does not necessarily follow that unconscious processes are relevant. Several alternative explanations deserve detailed logical and empirical consideration, if only because there are reasons for questioning the existence of unconscious processes in creative thinking.

Creativity in Dreams

One important question should be addressed before the discussion of unconscious thought processes is completed. This question concerns creative problem solving in dreams.

There are a number of reports of problem solving during dreams in the literature on creativity, of which Coleridge's is only one. Dreams involving mathematics are very rare. Hadamard discusses a mathematician's report of an experience of his mother and his mother's sister. The two were rivals in mathematics at school. One evening they worked unsuccessfully on a difficult geometry problem. During the night, one of the sisters began reciting the solution to the problem in a loud voice while still asleep. The other girl wrote down the solution, and reported it in class the next day. The girl who had *produced* the solution was not aware that she had had anything to do with it.

Reports of creative acts in dreams are fascinating, although difficult to verify. While it is obvious that a dreaming person is not conscious, it is not obvious that solving a problem in a dream is evidence for unconscious thought processes of the sort postulated by Poincaré. Poincaré's theory of unconscious processes assumes that the unconscious works by combining thoughts until some combination "pops" into consciousness and suggests a direction for solving the problem. If one could "listen in" to these unconscious processes at work, one might expect to hear random free associations as the unconscious put ideas together until it stumbled upon something good. In the example of the two sisters just discussed, however, the sleeping sister simply recited the completed proof. There is no evidence of her combining ideas together, nor is it clear what that report means in terms of Poincare's notion of unconscious thought processes. Furthermore, since the girl recited the completed proof, she must have worked out the proof some time earlier. There is no evidence that she worked out the proof in a dream, and we are left without any idea of where the proof came from. Since the two girls were rivals in mathematics, it is possible they independently continued thinking about the problem after they stopped working on it. It is also possible that the girl was awake briefly when she worked out the solution, but did not remember it later. Finally, it is important to note that this report is at least third hand—Hadamard relates a story told to him by a mathematician which concerns something that happened to the mathematician's mother when she was a young girl. No one involved was a psychologist. Surely this report is not worth much as scientific evidence.

One of the most famous examples of what is supposed to be a creative act occurring in a dream is Friedrich August von Kekule's discovery of the benzene ring. The benzene ring, a basic structure in organic chemistry, involves six carbon atoms that are connected in such a way that they form a ring. Kekule discovered this structure in what Koestler calls "probably the most important dream in history since Joseph's seven fat and seven lean cows." This incident occurred after Kekule had been working on the problem for a while, and in the following quote, Kekule briefly refers to his earlier work.

> I turned my chair to the fire and dozed. Again the atoms were gamboling before my eyes. This time the smaller groups kept modestly to the background. My mental eye, rendered more acute by repeated vision of this kind, could now distinguish larger structures, of manifold conformation; long rows, sometimes more closely fitted together; all twining and twisting in snakelike motion. But look! What was that? One of the snakes had seized hold of its own tail, and the form whirled mockingly before my eyes. As if by a flash of lightning I awoke . . . Let us learn to dream, gentlemen.

In the usual interpretation of this incident, two important aspects are mentioned: Kekule was dreaming when the discovery was made, and he was dreaming about snakes. However, there is some question as to whether either of these points is true. In the passage quoted above, the word "doze" is used by Kekule to refer to his state. The quote is translated from the German, however, and in the original Kekule may not have meant he was actually asleep. The German word, "Halbschlaf" (half-sleep), has also been translated as "reverie." This would mean that he was not really sleeping, but rather was lost in thought.

Additional evidence that Kekule was not literally asleep and dreaming is found in the following line of the above quote, in which he continues to say, "take care not to make our dreams known before they have been worked through by the wakened understanding." Albert Rothenberg, a psychiatrist who has done much research in the area of creative thinking, feels that Kekule may have been using "dream" figuratively, to mean something like adventurous thinking, as when one says "I'm dreaming about winning the Olympics."

So there seems to be a question whether this "most important dream in history . . ." was even a dream at all. This is similar to Schneider's question of whether Coleridge was dreaming when *Kubla Khan* was produced.

The content of Kekule's "dream," the snake biting its tail, has also impressed many, because it supposedly points to the importance of analogies in thinking. According to this view, scientific discovery often occurs when analogies are found between different things. Kekule's discovery, therefore, is assumed to depend on his having discovered the analogy between a snake biting its tail and a ring of carbon atoms. Once again, however, the question arises whether Kekule was imagining snakes at all. In the passage quoted above, Kekule first talks about rows of atoms "in *snakelike* motion" (my italics). Kekule obviously does not think those rows are snakes, because he says *snakelike*. Furthermore, when he then says that "one of the snakes had seized hold of its own tail," he is probably speaking figuratively. Because he just described the strings as snakelike, he then describes the closed ring as being a snake biting its own tail. However, his use of the term *snake* depends on his earlier use of *snakelike*.

This sort of figurative usage often occurs in ordinary speech. As an example, if I disapprovingly tell someone that he eats like a pig, I may tell him to stop oinking when he tries to dispute my remark. Though I do not literally mean he makes piglike noises, the remark is obviously meaningful in context. The same may have occurred with Kekule: he described the chains of atoms figuratively as snakes for ease of communication, and this later led him to describe a closed ring in a figurative way.

Based on this reinterpretation of Kekule's statements, one would say that Kekule first imagined a closed ring of atoms, then *described* it as a snake biting its tail. This is not to deny that Kekule's *visual imagination* was crucial to his discovery, but it does deny that a *visual analogy* between strings of atoms and snakes had anything to do with it. In addition, all this imagining probably did not take place in a dream.

Conclusions

This chapter was intended to raise doubts about the often-taken-for-granted idea that unconscious incubation is important in creativity. The theory of incubation was postulated because a number of creative individuals reported the occurrence of far-ranging leaps of thought during their creative work that seemed to be independent of conscious thought and environmental events. According to Poincaré, creativity involves the combining of ideas in the unconscious and the eventual transfer of potentially useful combinations to consciousness. The leap of thought a person experiences is due to suddenly becoming conscious of a previously unconscious idea. There are now a number of reasons to doubt the occurrence of such leaps of thought, however. First, such leaps are difficult, if not impossible, to demonstrate under controlled conditions. Second, many of the reports on which the unconscious theory is based are of questionable accuracy. Though it is not possible to analyze all subjective reports brought forth as "evidence" for unconscious thought processes in creative thinking, the detailed analysis of reports by Mozart, Coleridge, and Poincaré was intended to demonstrate the need for skepticism. Given the problems revealed in the reports discussed here, which are frequently cited in the psychological literature, one could say that the burden of proof now falls on those who propose subjective reports as support for a theory of unconscious processes in creative thinking.

Again, it must be emphasized that I am not claiming that human beings never carry out such tasks as typing, or writing, or driving automatically. Automatic processing of well-learned habits is one thing—unconscious incubation is quite another.

In conclusion, the notion of unconscious incubation in creative thinking is evidently not very strongly based on fact. It is simply a story that many people believe without consideration of its merits; in the face of contradictory results, however, it is a story that should be put aside.

3

THE "AHA!" MYTH

One important aspect of the traditional view of creativity is that creation occurs in flashes of insight, sometimes called "aha!" reactions. According to this view, the creative act involves suddenly "seeing" the solution to one's problem, and the sudden insight can involve a leap beyond one's experience. In this view, heavy reliance on past experience can actually interfere with creative problem solving.

The following problems help clarify what is involved in an "aha!" experience. 1) A man in a certain town in the United States married twenty women from the town. All the women are still alive, none has been divorced, the man is not a Mormon, and yet the man broke no law. How is that possible? 2) Yesterday, when I went to sleep, I turned off the light and then got into bed. My bed is located twenty feet from the light switch, and yet I got into bed before the room got dark. How is that possible? 3) Our basketball team won a game last week by the score of 73–49, and yet not one man on our team scored as much as a single point. How is that possible? 4) What five-letter word do all college graduates spell wrong?

These four problems are examples of what are sometimes called "insight" problems, because it is assumed that solving them requires a leap of insight. They are so designed that when one first reads them, they seem to be describing familiar situations: a man getting married, someone going to sleep at night, two teams of college men playing basketball, and students' problems spelling. If one uses one's knowledge to interpret these situations in an ordinary way, however, one will not solve the problems. The answers to the problems are: 1) the man is the minister who married the women to their husbands; 2) I went to sleep when it was still daylight; 3) our team is a women's basketball team; 4) the word is W-R-O-N-G. Furthermore, when given the solutions, especially after trying unsuccessfully to solve the problems for a while, one may experience a sudden "aha!" kind of reaction as one sees that these situations can in reality be interpreted in more than one way. Upon changing the way one interprets the problems they become trivially easy, but if one continues to try to apply one's knowledge to them they remain unsolveable. Thus, the leap needed to solve these problems will not come about if one insists on interpreting them on the basis of one's past experience.

These problems are taken from a recent book on problem solving by Martin Gardner, a mathematician who has published much on solving problems. Gardner suggests ways a reader can increase his or her chances of solving the problems in the book, and also become a better problem solver in general. These hints amount to a succinct outline of the "aha!" view of creative problem solving.

> This book is a careful selection of problems that seem difficult, and indeed are difficult if you go about trying to solve them in traditional ways. But if you can free your mind from standard problem solving techniques, you may be receptive to an "aha!" reaction that leads immediately to solution.

Several aspects of this quote are worth emphasizing. First, one's mind must be freed from standard, traditional problem solving techniques, that is, one must forget past experience in order to solve the problems. Second, if one can free one's mind from standard techniques, one may be receptive to an "aha!" reaction. This sounds very passive for the problem solver: sit still, free your mind, and an "aha!" reaction may happen to you. The person apparently does nothing, just hopes that something will happen. As in the "messenger of god" view, in which creative ideas are provided by the Muses, Gardner seems to feel that one does not have to *do* anything except be ready to receive the "aha!" reaction. Finally, the "aha!" reaction, if one is lucky enough to receive it, leads immediately to the solution of the problem. Again, little work is required once this reaction occurs—everything falls into place and the solution is found.

To sum up, this view of creativity maintains that if one can break away from the hold of past experience one may experience spontaneous solutions to problems. This view was fostered, at least in part, by work conducted by Gestalt psychologists in the early part of the twentieth century. This chapter traces the evolution of the "aha!" view, beginning with some of the early Gestalt studies that attempt to grapple with the phenomenon of creative problem solving. Research that has tried to test various predictions based on the "aha!" view is then discussed. This leads to a consideration of research from a number of different areas, which, contrary to the "aha!" view, points to the important role of problem-specific knowledge, or expertise, in solving problems. The chapter concludes with a discussion of when past experience interferes with problem solving and when it is necessary for successful problem solving.

It should be emphasized that there is no question that all of us have "aha!" experiences at various times in our lives. We may be trying unsuccessfully to think of a word in a crossword puzzle, when suddenly it is recalled with a rush of emotion. Or, we may be working on a problem unsuccessfully for a considerable amount of time, when the solution suddenly comes to us. Some readers may have experienced an "aha!" reaction when they tried to solve the four insight problems presented above. The issue is not whether such experiences occur, because there is no doubt that they do, but whether they are the result of leaps of the imagination, which can be interfered with by past experience.

Early Associationism

In the early twentieth century, associationism was the dominant psychological view on thinking. It held that solving a new problem depended on the transfer of associations from old situations to the new situation. This is one example of what the first chapter called the "nothing new" view of creativity, in which the issue of creative problem solving is dealt with by assuming that nothing a person ever does is truly creative. This view can be traced back to John Watson, who was one of the leaders in the development of behaviorism in the United States.

Basically, in Watson's view, a solution to a novel problem is assumed to come about because the new situation is similar in some critical way to one that preceded it. That is, even though the situation is essentially new, it contains familiar elements. Because of this similarity, old associations are *transferred* or *generalized* to the new situation, and the novel problem is solved. This view argues that novel problems are solved because they are not really novel but are in fact familiar situations in slightly different clothes. According to this view, if a new situation were not similar to a previous one, the organism could only behave randomly. As an example of this assumed randomness, Watson claimed that poets produce new poems by randomly putting words together until they accidentally find a pattern they like. According to Watson's view, a poet's creating a poem is like a monkey randomly pressing typewriter keys and accidentally producing a word.

Evidence to support this theory came from Edward Thorndike's experiments in which cats placed in novel situations had to perform some response in order to get food (that is, one could say that the animals had to solve a problem in order to get food). In one situation, the hungry animal was put in a small cage, with food visible outside. The animal had to learn to pull a string to open the door. In another situation a vertical pole in the center of the cage had to be pushed aside by the hungry animal in order to trigger a door-opening mechanism. Thorndike found that the animals only very gradually learned what they had to do to get out of the cages. They showed no "intelligence" or "reasoning ability," and performed in an essentially trial-and-error manner until they acquired the relevant experience. Only then were the cats able to respond efficiently. Thorndike concluded that acquiring relevant experience is crucial in problem solving, and that such experience is acquired and put to use a little piece at a time.

The Gestalt View

In response to this associationistic view, the Gestalt psychologists argued that creative thinking, or productive thinking as they called it, entailed going beyond one's past experience to work out each new problem as an independent experience. These psychologists wished to show that one could solve problems for which one had no specific knowledge or experience simply by considering what the real difficulty was and how to overcome it. One did not have to behave randomly in a novel situation. "Gestalt" is translated from German to mean "form," reflecting the Gestalt psychologists' interest in *perceptual forms,* those factors that determine the forms we perceive when we look around our environment. The Gestalt psychologists also thought that problem solving and creative thinking were related to perception.

In their analysis of problem solving, Gestalt psychologists made a distinction between *reproductive* thought, which simply involves the reproduction or recall of past experience, and *productive* thought, which involves creation of something truly novel. Two important examples of the Gestalt view of thinking are found in Köhler's word on problem solving in apes, and Wertheimer's work with children learning to find the area of geometric figures.

Wolfgang Köhler, a leader of the Gestalt movement, spent World War I on the island of Tenerife, where he studied problem solving in a colony of apes. In direct response to Thorndike's work, Köhler set out to show that animals could demonstrate intelligence while solving novel problems and that they were not limited to associations previously acquired in similar situations. One difference between Köhler's experiments and those of Thorndike was that Köhler laid all the component parts out in front of the animal. For example, in one situation a banana was placed outside the animal's cage beyond reach. A stick was placed just outside the cage within view, and available for use as a "rake." Köhler felt that if all the components of the situation were available to the animal it would be able to work out a solution, despite its lack of relevant experience. This working-out of the solution would occur because of perceptual processes, which the Gestalt psychologists consider to be very important in problem solving. According to the Gestalt view, if the stick is in the animal's field of view while it looks for a way to reach the banana, the visible length of the stick will cause the animal to realize that it can serve as a means of lengthening its arm. This realization is thought to occur because of the way in which the situation is perceived, which is assumed to be relatively independent of past experience.

Köhler found that some subjects did do things like put two short sticks together to make a long one to rake in a banana from outside the cage. In another situation, one of Köhler's apes piled several boxes on top of each other, ladder-like, in order to reach a banana hanging from the top of the cage. According to the Gestalt view, if the situation is set up right, things "click" and the subject sees the solution to the problem. This idea of "seeing" the solution is important because, as mentioned earlier, Gestalt psychologists emphasize the importance of perceptual processes in thinking. According to the Gestalt view, problems arise when the situation is organized in such a way that the important perceptual relations among the objects are kept hidden. For example, consider a situation in which an ape is trying to reach a banana beyond his grasp; though there is a potentially useful stick *behind the ape,* it cannot be seen while the ape looks at the banana. In such a situation, the ape never thinks of using the stick because the connection between the need to extend his reach and the length of the stick is not seen.

Max Wertheimer, another leader of the Gestalt movement, studied thinking in children extensively, although much of his work was done relatively informally. Wertheimer's work was very influential in shaping the view that past experience is not really necessary for, and can even interfere with, creative thinking. In several situations, Wertheimer presented school children with problems in order to study the importance of past experience in problem solving. In one situation, shown in Figure 3.1a, children were first taught to find the area of a rectangle by filling it with small squares and then counting the squares. Once

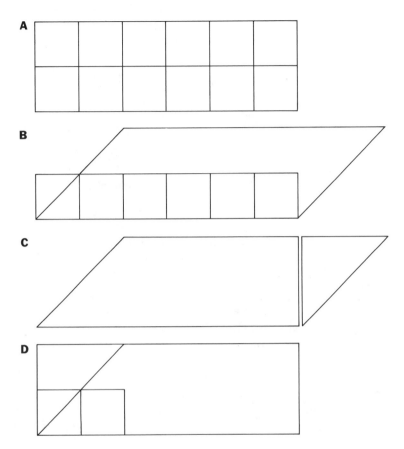

Figure 3.1
An insightful solution to Wertheimer's parallelogram problem.

they could do this, Wertheimer made the problem more difficult by asking them to find the area of a parallelogram, as shown in Figure 3.1b. Some children simply gave up when they saw the new figure and said the area could not be determined; others immediately asked the teacher for help; and still others tried, unsuccessfully, to fit the squares into the new shape, as in Figure 3.1b.

Though Wertheimer does not say how many, a few children produced truly creative solutions, an example of which is shown in Figure 3.1c and d. This child said "It's troublesome *here* and *here*. [Pointing to the two nonrectangular ends of the parallelogram.] I could make it right here . . . but . . ." Then the child suddenly asked for a pair of scissors, saying "What is bad there is just what is needed here." She then cut the parallelogram, as shown in Figure 3.1c, and moved the smaller piece to the other end to make a rectangle, as shown in Figure 3.1d. Thus, this child produced a creative solution in what seems to be an "aha!" reaction, or a leap of insight. Furthermore, Wertheimer argued, this solution did not depend on the child's past experience, but rather depended on her reasoning out the difficulties that arose as she tried to solve this particular problem. According to Wertheimer, the child's ability to reason through the situation was more important than her specific past experience in producing that creative solution.

> It is my impression as a result of such experiments that children can be able to find out, by actual reasonable working at a problem, just what is needed—without special previous experience. They find the needed experiences for themselves, in a reasonable way.

Even more interestingly, Wertheimer claimed that creative thinking can be interfered with by a strong dependence on specific past experience. He was concerned especially about the effect that drill in school had on creative problem solving.

> It seems to me, although I do not have sufficient quantitative data on this point, that the ability to produce such fine, genuine [thought] processes often decreases considerably in school children when they become accustomed to drill.

Drill involves going over and over a particular situation, or small group of situations, until the student knows the correct answer, and Wertheimer believed that one was better off without relevant past experience because of the tendencies to try and apply it where it is not really useful. An example of this is when the children in Wertheimer's experiment tried to find the area of the parallelogram by simply transferring the method then used with the rectangle, despite the fact that the little squares did not fit inside the parallelogram. Wertheimer's view also is relevant to adults who have "drilled" in many situations throughout their lives; it implies that adults may be more "rigid" and less creative than children are.

In summary, Wertheimer felt that a strong reliance on past experience could interfere with creative problem solving. In order to break away from past experience and produce a truly novel solution to a problem, one had to analyze the specific difficulties of the problem one was dealing with. If one "thought out the gaps" in the problem, a solution would fall into place.

The Flash of Insight and Spontaneous Restructuring

In order to explain the origin of creative solutions, such as those observed by Köhler and Wertheimer, the Gestalt psychologists began with the idea that creative problem solving is similar to perception in important ways. When one looks at the Necker cube in Figure 3.2, for example, one usually sees a cube with a specific orientation. If one continues looking, however, the cube may suddenly reverse itself in depth and essentially flip inside out. This reversal of the cube is called *spontaneous restructuring* for two reasons. First, the reversal of the cube indicates that one's perception has been restructured, in the sense that the parts of the cube change in their relation to each other. If it is first seen as projecting down to the left, for example, then when it reverses, the face that was in the back comes to the front, and so on. Furthermore, this reversal and restruc-

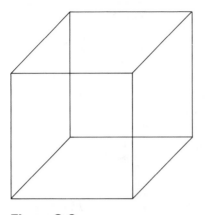

Figure 3.2
The Necker cube.

turing are thought to occur independently of one's experiences, and so are spontaneous as far as the psychologist is concerned.

In order to explain spontaneous restructuring in perceptual situations like the reversible cube, the Gestalt psychologists assume it is the result of the way the brain functions. The person's viewing an object in the world sets up a certain pattern of excitation in the visual area of the brain. In some cases, the particular pattern of excitation is such that it spontaneously changes into another pattern. When this happens, one's perception of the world is suddenly restructured, as when the cube is seen as reversing.

The Gestalt psychologists claim that spontaneous restructuring may occur in a similar way in problem solving. The problem solver suddenly sees the problem situation in a new way, and this new perception can be accompanied by a novel way of solving the problem, and a feeling of "aha!" An example of such spontaneous restructuring in problem solving is seen in the behavior of Köhler's ape who first sat quietly, then piled boxes like a ladder to reach a banana. According to the Gestalt view, this sudden emergence of a new solution type (the animal had not piled up boxes before) is due to a spontaneous restructuring, similar to that which occurs in perception. With this restructuring the boxes are perceived as something to climb on, and so a new solution results. Furthermore, when the Necker cube reverses, it does so completely, not in parts. The same thing happens when a problem situation is spontaneously restructured—all the parts and their relations change. The problem solver suddenly achieves a new understanding of the parts of the problem and their relations. This is why the new solution is produced smoothly and not in fits and starts.

To summarize, the "aha!" view of problem solving evolved out of the Gestalt psychologists' interest in perceptual processes. They theorize that under certain circumstances a problem situation might undergo spontaneous restructuring, which produces the sudden appearance of a new solution type, and with it an "aha!" reaction, a feeling of sudden insight. According to this view, if a person can work through a problem, no special knowledge is needed to produce a solution. All that is required is that he or she consider the situation in the right way. Of course, the Gestalt psychologists acknowledged that problem solving does not occur completely independently of past experience. For example, the little girl who solved Wertheimer's parallelogram problem by cutting off the end of the parallelogram knew how to use scissors, though she had never used them to transform a parallelogram into a rectangle. This use of scissors was something she produced herself by working through the problem. Thus, the difference between the associationistic and Gestalt views concerns the emphasis placed on past experience. The Gestalt psychologists concentrate on the production of novel solutions to problems, solutions that do not seem to depend on any specific past experience.

An Example of Fixation Due to Past Experience

According to the "aha!" view of creative problem solving, a person's inability to produce a novel solution to a problem is usually due to their being stuck in the rut of past experience. Though Wertheimer deplored the disappearance of the "fine, genuine [thought] processes" when school children are exposed to drill, all of life can be seen as "drill," and our habitual ways of doing things can trap us when a novel problem occurs. According to the "aha!" view, a person can sometimes become *fixated* on past experience and mistakenly rely on it to solve a problem when it is not really relevant. This blind reliance on past experience may be so strong that one is unable to solve what would be a simple problem if one could open one's eyes to the problem itself. The Gestalt psychologists who studied problem solving spent much time demonstrating the negative effects brought about by fixation on past experience.

One well-studied situation that demonstrates the negative effect of past experience is presented in Table 3.1. Readers who are not familiar with this situation should work through Table 3.1 before going further.

Though they look similar initially, there are three different kinds of water-jar problems in Table 3.1. The first five problems are all solved using a single, relatively complicated method (B-A-C-C). People usually solve most of the first five problems, especially the last few, because of the repetition of the B-A-C-C solution. Though problems 6 and 7 look similar to problems 1–5, they differ in that they can be solved in two ways, either by the B-A-C-C solution, or by a simpler solution using only two jars. After working through the first five problems, most people solve problems 6 and 7 using the complicated B-A-C-C solution and never even see the simpler solution. Problem 8 also looks like the preceding problems, but differs in still another way—it is the first problem in the series for which the B-A-C-C solution will not work. The solution to problem 8 is simple and, ordinarily most people would have little trouble solving it. If a group of subjects first solves problems 1–7, however, a significant proportion of them will have trouble with problem 8 and some will not solve it.

To summarize, when subjects work through a series of problems such as that in Table 3.1, in which a simple solution is repeated for the first several prob-

Table 3.1
Water-jar problems

You are given jars labelled A, B, and C, and an unlimited amount of water. Use the three jars in combination to produce the required amount of water. Assume that you cannot estimate amounts: any jars must be filled to the top.

Problem	Jars (capacity in quarts)			Required	Solution
	A	B	C		
Practice	29	3	—	20 quarts	A-B-B-B★ (Fill A, empty water into B three times; 20 quarts left in A.)
Practice	21	127	3	100	B-A-C-C or B-9C
1	14	163	25	99	B-A-2C
2	30	57	4	19	
3	18	43	10	5	
4	9	42	6	21	
5	20	59	4	31	
6	23	49	3	20	
7	15	39	3	18	
8	28	76	3	25	

★To be read as: A minus B, minus B, minus B; or, A minus 3B.
SOURCE: From R. Weisberg (1980). *Memory, thought, and behavior.* New York: Oxford University Press.

lems, they can have trouble with those that appear later. This trouble can be of two sorts. First, relying on their past experience, they use the complicated solution on problems that can be solved more simply, thereby wasting time and effort. Second, they may sometimes try the previously successful method even though it is not relevant, and thus be unable to solve a problem that "nonexperienced" subjects solve easily. In other words, by relying on past experience in a situation where it does not apply, the experienced person is completely unsuccessful. One could say, as regards Table 3.1, that past success with the B-A-C-C solution "blinds" one to the simpler solutions for problems 6–8.

This type of situation is called a "problem solving set." Subjects acquire a *set* or become *fixated* on the previously successful method and cannot break away from it to approach each new problem as a unique situation. In the Gestalt view, this inability to approach each problem as a unique situation is often what keeps people from exhibiting creativity.

This theory has been applied broadly by Gestalt-influenced psychologists to explain problem solving, or lack of it, in many different situations. The next section examines research intending to test this theory. As can be seen, however, it provides little support for the Gestalt view of the importance of fixation.

Testing the Gestalt Notion of Fixation

Over the years, psychologists have discussed a number of other problems that are assumed to demonstrate the general importance of fixation in problem solving. These problems are called "insight" problems, because solving them is thought to require a sudden restructuring of the problem, which is accompanied by the sensation of a flash of insight. The best-known of these problems is presented in Figure 3.3. Readers who are not familiar with it should work through the instructions in Figure 3.3 before reading further.

According to Gestalt theory, the nine-dot problem in Figure 3.3 is really very easy. The reason most people fail to solve it is that their past experience interferes in the form of *assumptions* they make about the problem. People assume that the lines they draw must stay within the boundaries of the square formed by the dots, but nowhere in the problem does it say that the lines are limited in any way. Fixation on the square formed by the dots, presumably brought about by past experience, makes it impossible to solve the problem. If this fixation could be broken and the problem approached on its own terms, however, the solution would be trivially easy, or so the Gestalt theory states.

The nine-dot problem is at least vaguely familiar to most of us because it often appears on "creativity tests" of various sorts, in seminars designed to teach creative thinking, and even in magazines and on place mats in restaurants. The ubiquity of this problem is a graphic example of the triumph of the Gestalt view of creativity in our society, although the place mat designers probably know little or nothing about Gestalt psychology. Wherever the nine-dot problem appears, it is accompanied by a discussion of how most people are not creative in solving it because they get stuck on the square; if they could just move beyond the square shape, the discussion continues, creative thought could emerge and the problem would suddenly and easily be solved.

Although many explicitly or implicitly accept the Gestalt fixation explanation of why the nine-dot problem is so difficult, until relatively recently there were no experimental results to support it. However, it seems relatively easy to test the Gestalt view. If fixation on the boundaries of the square interferes with finding the solution, then getting people to go outside the square should break the fixation, and make the solution readily apparent. According to Gestalt theory, the nine-dot problem is difficult solely because of the assumptions made about it; if these assumptions are dropped, the solution to the problem will become clear. Two studies, by Clarke Burnham and Kenneth Davis and Joseph Alba and me, tested this assumption and found no support for the Gestalt view. Subjects were told that the only way to solve the nine-dot problem was to draw lines outside the square. Burnham and Davis told subjects to go outside the square initially; Weisberg and Alba let subjects work on the problem first before giving them the hint to go outside the square, hoping that this would increase their acceptance of the hint.

The two studies produced nearly identical results. Once told that they could not solve the problem without going outside the square, essentially all subjects went outside the square. That is, they tried to use the hint. According to the

Fig. 3.3

The dot problem. Connect all nine dots with four straight lines, without lifting your pencil from the paper.

Gestalt view, going outside the square should eliminate the fixation and allow restructuring to occur, which in turn should make the problem trivially easy. However, the problem did not become trivially easy—only 20–25 percent of the subjects told to go outside the square actually solved the problem. The Gestalt view holds that once the fixation is broken the solution either appears whole in a flash of insight or is produced smoothly as one step leads to another. In neither study were such results seen. The few subjects who did solve the problem after receiving the hint took a long time to do so. In addition, Weisberg and Alba's record of the successive solution attempts their subjects produced showed that all responded to the hint by drawing random lines outside the square. Only gradually did they "home in" on the solution. Nor did any show evidence of knowing what they were doing beforehand as they worked out the solution. The best evidence for such lack of foresight is demonstrated by several subjects who simply drew a line outside the boundary of the square and said "Okay, I'm outside the square. Now what do I do?" Weisberg and Alba also examined several other problems in which fixation is assumed to interfere with solution and found no evidence to support the Gestalt view.

One might object to the above results and feel that because the hint provides rather vague information it is not surprising that it helps so little. One might also argue that the solution comes slowly in this problem because multiple restructurings are required. Going outside the square, after all, is only the first of several necessary steps that must be taken. Claims that multiple restructurings are necessary to solve the nine-dot problem, however, tend to dilute the Gestalt theory to a point where it is basically no different than Thorndike's trial-and-error view. Since such restructuring presumably would occur as the subject worked on the problem, it would be similar to the process Thorndike talked of.

In summary, the Gestalt view that a solution can occur in an "Aha!" experience if one simply breaks away from past experience has been attractive because it emphasizes the power of the individual's reasoning processes. It also implies that we all could be creative problem solvers, in any domain, if we only gave ourselves the chance. Attractive as this view may be, however, the results of several experimental studies lead one to question it.

Expertise in Problem Solving

Contrary to the "aha!" view, the results discussed so far indicate that people need relatively specific knowledge about a given problem if they are to be successful in solving it. Additional evidence supports this view.

Köhler's findings concerning insightful problem solving in apes were some of the early discoveries to influence the Gestalt theorists. Several of Köhler's subjects produced novel solutions to problems, presumably without any directly relevant past experience. This led to the idea that the perceptual structure of a situation could result in all the pieces "falling into place" so long as the relevant objects were available for scrutiny. Given the importance of Köhler's findings in the history of psychology, it is important to raise the question of the role of past experience in the performance of Köhler's apes. The animals in Köhler's experiments were captured, not raised from birth in captivity, leaving open the possibility that past experience played a role in their "insightful" behavior.

In order to examine this possibility, Herbert Birch raised apes from birth and thus possessed detailed knowledge about their experiences with sticks. He presented five of these naive animals with the "hoe" problem shown in Figure 3.4. The hungry animal can see both an out-of-reach piece of food and a potentially useful stick simultaneously as it unsuccessfully reaches for the food. Köhler's positive results using problems of this sort were taken as strong support for the Gestalt view that perceptual processes are important in producing creative thought.

However, none of Birch's naive subjects used the stick in a way which supported the Gestalt view. One subject never touched the stick in 30 minutes' work on the problem. Three other subjects picked up the stick and angrily threw it away, as if they felt that the stick were interfering with their solving the problem. Finally, one subject accidentally hit the stick, causing the food to move. He then deliberately tried to move the food with the stick and when he was successful, pulled it to him. In no case did the solution unfold in a series of related steps as the Gestalt theory claims. Even though the various visual elements in the situation were "properly" arranged, Birch's apes showed no insight concerning how the stick could be used as an extension of their arms. This indicates that the insight shown by Köhler's animals may have been much more dependent on specific past experience he realized.

Additional evidence also indicates that the capacity to behave insightfully depends on extensive experience in that sort of situation. Harry Harlow studied the ability of monkeys to solve two-choice discrimination problems, such as those shown at the top of Figure 3.5. Although intelligent animals, monkeys perform very poorly, in a fumbling, trial and error manner, when they are first given such a problem. The animal may choose one stimulus and get food, but then make a

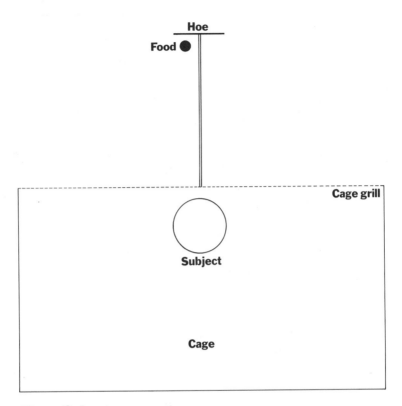

Figure 3.4
Birch's "hoe" problem.

mistake and pick the other stimulus; it only gradually learns to always choose the correct stimulus.

Harlow gave his subjects a long series of more than 300 discrimination problems in which the stimuli changed from problem to problem. By the time the animals finished the series they were solving problems insightfully. That is, with each new problem, the animal first picked one of the two stimuli at random, since it could not know which stimulus hid the food. Once the first choice was made, however, the animal never made a mistake. If the initial choice were correct, the animal picked that stimulus exclusively from then on; if it were incorrect, the animal immediately picked the other stimulus and never returned to the incorrect stimulus. Thus, at the end of the series, the animal behaved with insight and solved the problem without fumbling. Harlow called this ability a "learning set." These animals developed a learning set for discrimination problems. His results are important because they bridge the gap between Thorndike's trial-and-error results and Köhler's insightful animals.

At the beginning of training Harlow's subjects learned only with difficulty. Although the animal saw the food under the same stimulus several times, this information had little effect. After 300 problems, on the other hand, the same

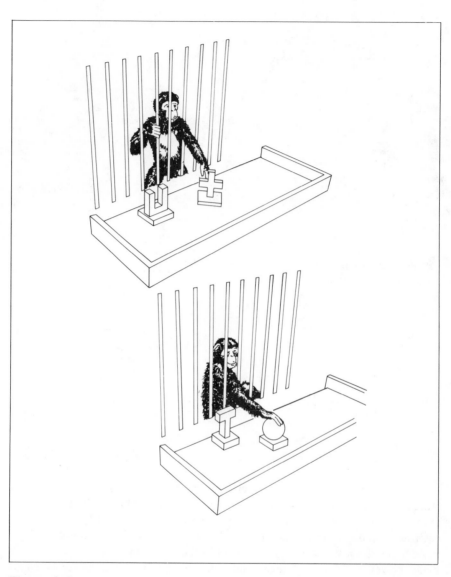

Figure 3.5

Harlow's two-choice discrimination problems. (From Harlow and Harlow, 1949. Learning to think. Copyright © 1949 by Scientific American, Inc. All rights reserved).

animal was very sensitive to perceptual information. It only needed to see where the food was once and it would choose that stimulus from then on. Though these two animals, the beginner and the expert, seem to be basically different, if a single animal is observed throughout the series, one sees that it only gradually learns to make complete use of the available information. In summary, Harlow's work indicates that insightful solutions of even seemingly simple problems depend on much experience with problems of that sort. Problems that appear to be trivially simple may only seem so because of the knowledge one brings to them. As Harlow's work demonstrates, one should not underestimate the difficulties an inexperienced problem solver confronts in a problem situation.

When Does Past Experience Interfere with Problem Solving?

As we have seen, "insightful" problem solving depends first and foremost on extensive expertise in the domain in question. This conclusion is essentially contrary to the Gestalt view, which tends to downplay the role of past experience and even assume that it can interfere with problem solving. Furthermore, the results on expertise reviewed in the discussion on fixation seem to contradict those from the water-jar studies presented in Table 3.1, because the latter indicate that in some domains extensive past experience can lead to difficulties solving new problems.

In order to resolve this seeming contradiction, it is worthwhile to consider briefly the structure of the problems in a typical water-jar experiment, such as those in Table 3.1. These problems appear to be very similar on the surface: all have three jars, the largest jar is in the middle, the middle-sized jar is on the left, and the smallest jar is on the right. Even though all eight problems appear to be alike, and even though the first five have the same solution, the last three problems are quite different from the others. The differences are not apparent until the problem solver tries to work them out, and then finds, for example, that the last problem cannot be solved with the same solution that has worked for all the others.

It is important to emphasize the deceptive nature of water-jar problems. The subject is led to assume that they are one sort of problem, that their appearance is meaningful, but this turns out to be incorrect. Like certain paintings that are made so realistically that one wonders at first if actual objects are involved, only careful observation reveals the true nature of the situation. If this analysis is correct, water-jar problems are not truly representative of problem-solving situations. In the great majority of problems individuals face, the new situation is similar to an old one and knowledge of the old is at least partly relevant to the new situation. In such cases, one makes advances in solving the new problem by applying one's knowledge. If a mechanic raises the hood of a car, for example, and sees what looks like an engine, it is an an engine. If a computer programmer must write a program to add numbers, then old programs that add numbers will be helpful in writing the new one. If this is so, then the water-jar situation is not at all representative of situations which demand creative thinking. Further evidence to support the crucial role of expertise in creative thinking is presented in the Chapter 6 discussion of scientific creativity, and the Chapter 7 discussion of creativity in the arts.

To summarize, past experience can interfere with creative problem solving, but only in highly artificial "trick" situations in which similarities in appearance among problems only hide differences. Though it is possible for one to be "tricked" in such situations, I believe that most situations calling for creative problem solving do not involve hidden tricks and pitfalls. Conclusions based on water-jar problems, therefore, are not relevant to most problem solving situations.

Conclusions: Are there Leaps of Insight?

The notion that creativity occurs in leaps of insight is one of the most widely believed aspects of the traditional view of creativity. This chapter has raised questions about the "Aha!" view of creativity in general and about the Gestalt view in particular.

The Gestalt view of problem solving and creativity is based on the belief that productive thinking (the creation of something novel in order to solve a problem) is not directly based on past experience. According to the Gestalt view, the crucial factor involved in productive thinking is that the person attempt to examine the specific problem as deeply as possible, in order to determine just what the difficulty is, and how to overcome it. Furthermore, according to this view, a reliance on past experience may result in a person's inability to solve a problem. Evidence supporting this view is varied. Investigations of problem solving in both humans and animals indicate that new problems can sometimes be solved in an integrated manner, without the blind trial-and-error reported by Thorndike. There are also experimental demonstrations of the negative effects of past experience on problem solving.

Detailed analysis of various aspects of the "Aha!" view indicates that there is actually very little support for the notion that creative solutions to problems come about in flashes of insight, independently of past experience. The "insightful" problem solving behavior of some of the apes studied by Köhler is probably based on uncontrolled past experience. Harlow's work on learning sets demonstrate how "insightful" behavior in animals, in one situation at least, is the result of extensive experience in that sort of situation. Similar results with humans show that in order to achieve anything like insightful behavior, the person must be familiar with the kind of problem being considered.

To summarize, although the "Aha!" view has a large following, there seems to be very little reason to believe that solutions to novel problems come about in leaps of insight. This conclusion is also supported by the negative results concerning unconscious processes in creativity, discussed in Chapter 2. On the whole, it seems reasonable to conclude that people create solutions to new problems by starting with what they know and later modify it to meet the specific problem at hand. At every step of the way, the process involves a small movement away from what is known, and even these small tentative movements into the unknown are firmly anchored in past experience.

4

THE MYTH OF
DIVERGENT THINKING

Our society has a great interest in self-improvement, and one area in which many of us seek improvement is the area of creative thinking. Courses are available that teach creative thinking, and consulting companies provide seminars in creative thinking for industry. As examples of the breadth of interest in increasing creative capacity, during the last part of 1983, articles concerning creative-thinking courses appeared in *The New York Times, Readers' Digest, Vogue,* and various business publications. *Omni* magazine recently published a profile of Edward De Bono, a leader in the creativity training movement and one who is constantly traveling around the world giving seminars. The title of the article, "The professor who teaches presidents to think," provides ample evidence of the importance of this movement in our society. The Venezuelan government recently initiated a program whereby *every school child in Venezuela* will be exposed to De Bono's methods of teaching creative thinking.

The main purpose of the present chapter is to review theory and research concerned with the question of whether individuals can be taught to think creatively. The chapter introduces the concept of creative thinking that most of the creative thinking programs are based on, a concept that assumes there are at least two types of thinking: divergent and convergent thinking. Also included in this concept is the assumption that divergent thinking (sometimes called lateral thinking) is especially important in creativity. Following the discussion of these different types of thinking is a description of how a typical course might attempt to facilitate creative thinking, by increasing a person's capacity for divergent thinking. The discussion then centers on the use of the brainstorming method to facilitate divergent thinking. This is followed by a review of research that has examined the effectiveness of brainstorming. The chapter concludes with a discussion of why brainstorming is not an effective method for facilitating creative thinking. The implications of these findings broaden our understanding of creative thinking, especially as it concerns the question of whether extraordinary thought processes are involved in creativity.

The best introduction to the creativity training movement is to take some creativity tests. Figure 4.1 includes five different tests used to asses different kinds of thinking. Working through these problems will make the following discussion more meaningful.

Problem 1   List all of the questions you can think of concerning the figure shown below. Ask all of the questions you need to know for sure what is happening. Do not ask questions that can be answered just by looking at the drawing. (Give yourself three minutes to list your questions.)

Problem 2   Suppose that all humans were born with six fingers on each hand instead of five. List all the consequences or implications that you can think of. (Give yourself three minutes.)

Problem 3   List as many white, edible things as you can in three minutes.

Problem 4   List all the words that you can think of in response to *mother*. (Give yourself 3 minutes.)

Problem 5   List all the uses that you can think of for a *brick*. (Give yourself 3 minutes.)

Fig. 4.1

Some creativity problems. (Adapted from E. P. Torrance, 1968, "Examples and rationales of test tasks for assessing creative abilities," *Journal of Creative Behavior* 2 [3], published by The Creative Education Foundation, Buffalo, New York. Used with permission.)

Two Types of Thinking

Although a number of different methods for teaching creative thinking have been developed over the years, they share one general idea. Creative problem solving is assumed to involve a series of stages, among which are consideration of the problem, generation of possible solutions, and evaluation of solutions. The main emphasis of most teaching methods is the stage of generating possible solutions, or what could be called "idea finding." The basic assumption is that one increases the chances of creatively solving a problem by producing many ideas. Once an idea is generated, it can then be tried to see if it will work. According to this view, the difficulty is in the initial generation of ideas, and that is where the teaching methods come in. Thus, at least two types of thinking are assumed to be occurring here, one involved in producing ideas, the other involved in applying them to the problem and evaluating the outcomes. The first is "free-form" associative thinking, while the evaluative thinking is standard, ordinary logical thinking.

Edward De Bono makes clear the distinction between these two types of thinking.

> Everyone recognizes the extreme usefulness of logical thinking but many people are unaware that new ideas come about in a different way. . . . The logical way of using the mind is tremendously effective at developing ideas once they have come about, but it is not so good at generating the ideas.

De Bono believes that logical thinking is not helpful in creative thinking, that is, in generating new ideas, because it "follows the most obvious line," that is, we try to solve problems using our past experience, our "tried and true" methods. According to De Bono, many problems, including presumably the most important ones, require a fresh viewpoint, that is not provided by ordinary "tried and true" logical thinking. Though De Bono uses the term "lateral" thinking to refer to thinking that generates new ways of approaching problems, I shall use the term divergent thinking because it is more widely used in the literature.

> Everyone has come across the type of problem which seems impossible to solve and then turns out to have an obvious answer. These are the problems that elicit the remark: 'Why didn't I think of that before?' Many inventions are obvious once someone else has thought of them. . . . Lateral thinking seeks to get away from the patterns that are leading one in a definite direction and to move sideways by re-forming the patterns.

De Bono is one of many individuals who have developed methods designed to help the thinker produce novel ideas in response to a problem, and thereby generate a fresh way of looking at it that results in a creative solution. These methods are designed to facilitate one's breaking away from old habits of thinking and allow one to produce ideas in response to a problem that one would ordinarily not produce. This in turn is intended to present the thinker with new combinations of ideas or fresh ways of viewing the problem.

Other writers in this area have also concentrated on idea finding and have made a distinction similar to that made by De Bono. James Adams, in a well-known guide to creative thinking, says this about what he hopes to do in his book.

> We will be concentrating on conceptualization, or the process by which one has ideas. This process is a key one in problem-solving, since the more creative concepts you have to choose from the better.

According to Adams, one can have difficulties solving problems, that is, difficulties thinking creatively, because the capacity for conceptualization becomes blocked in various ways. Adams incorporates the ideas of De Bono and others in his discussion of the various sorts of blocks he thinks can occur and how he thinks they should be overcome. Adams's view is presented in detail in a later section.

The emphasis on fostering idea production can also be seen in the *synectics* method developed by William Gordon. The word *synectics,* from the Greek, means the joining together of different and apparently irrelevant elements. Though the method has emphasized the joining together of diverse people into effective problem solving groups, it also applies to individuals. Gordon, like many others, emphasizes the "underlying, nonrational, free-associative concepts that flow under the articulated surface phenomena." This is contrasted with ordinary thinking in which one tries to apply past experience to a new problem.

> It is the function of the mind, when presented with a problem, to attempt to make the strange familiar by means of analysis. The human organism is basically conservative, and any strange thing is threatening to it. When faced with strangeness the mind attempts to engorge this strangeness by forcing it into an acceptable pattern or changing its (the mind's) private geometry of bias to make room for the strangeness. The mind compares the given strangeness with data previously known and in terms of these data converts the strangeness into familiarity. . . . . The process of making the strange familiar, if used alone, yields a variety of superficial solutions: but basic novelty demands a fresh viewpoint, a new way of looking at the problem. Most problems are not new. The challenge is to view the problem in a new way. This new viewpoint in turn embodies the potential for a new basic solution.

Once again the distinction is made between logically applying one's past experience to a problem, and another way of thinking that is important in creativity: nonrational and free-associative thinking.

This view has spread far beyond psychologists and business people interested solely in creativity. Paul Watzlawick, John Weakland, and Richard Fisch have proposed a view of psychotherapy which incorporates an analysis of the thinking process that is very similar to the distinction between logical and lateral thinking. According to this view, a therapist tries to resolve a patient's problem by producing a change in the patient, and sometimes change is very difficult to bring about. One of the reasons that people go into therapy, according to Watzlawick et al., is because the methods they are using to try to alleviate their problems are only making things worse. The task of the therapist, therefore, is to devise a new method with which to approach the problem. These new methods are often not the result of ordinary logical thinking.

> On the one hand, although logic and common sense offer excellent solutions when they work, who has not had the frustrating experience of doing his very best in these terms, only to see things going from bad to worse? On the other hand, every once in a while we experience some "illogical" and surprising but welcome change in a troublesome stalemate.

Again we see a distinction between the logical and the creative. Watzlawick et al. propose a number of methods whereby therapists and others concerned with changing behavior (e.g., school psychologists) can learn to produce the illogical but welcome change.

To summarize, theorists from a number of different areas have emphasized that two different kinds of thinking are involved in creativity. The most important of these, which is assumed to be critical in producing novel approaches to problems, involves not logical thinking, but thinking that is "freer" and allows the problem solver to break away from old habits of thought. Courses in improving creativity are designed to foster this kind of thinking.

Guilford's Analysis of Creative Thinking

The creativity training industry developed largely independently of scientific psychology, partly because most psychologists in the 1950s and 1960s were not interested in creative problem solving, and were therefore not in a position to assist business leaders who wished to increase the creative thinking capacity of their employees. An exception to this were psychologists involved in the mental-testing movement, who were sympathetic to the need to develop ways of measuring human creativity. A leader in this movement was J. P. Guilford, who helped develop tests to measure various aspects of creativity, and whose theorizing supported the notion that two sorts of thinking were involved.

Guilford's 1950 presidential address to the American Psychological Association expressed dismay over the "appalling" neglect of creativity by psychologists, and attributed much of this neglect to their interest in learning in lower animals. In order to help stimulate interest in the subject, Guilford presented his own theory as a set of hypotheses concerning the specific abilities important in creative thinking. The next step would be to develop psychological tests to determine whether the hypothesized abilities actually occurred. The last step would be to determine if these abilities were indeed related to creative accomplishments of various sorts. Guilford assumed that individuals possess *traits,* that is, enduring psychological properties, and that some of these are related to creative capacity. The hypothesized traits are measured by appropriate tests. The tests in Figure 4.1 are based on Guilford's theorizing.

Guilford theorized first that individuals differ in how *sensitive* they are to problems present in given area of investigation. As an example, two research scientists might examine a report, but only one might see a problem in the results. Obviously, only this scientist would think further about the results and thus have a chance of producing a creative solution to the problem. Since the other scientist does not even see that there is a problem, there is no chance for creative thinking to occur on his or her part.

As a possible test for this trait, Guilford suggests asking a person to name common household objects, and then to list things that are wrong with them or that could be improved. Another possible test is to give people short expository paragraphs and ask them to question anything suggested by the material. Those who perform well on such tests (that is, those who list many things or ask many questions) are assumed to possess one trait important for certain kinds of creative thinking. Problems 1 and 2 in Figure 4.1 test for sensitivity to problems.

Guilford hypothesized that individuals also differ in the ease with which they produce ideas. Those who are capable of producing many ideas in a given amount of time, who are *fluent,* are more likely to produce significant ideas. To test for fluency, an examinee might be asked to name, within a time limit, as many objects as possible possessing some specified property, for example, white edible things or liquids that burn. Another test for fluency would be to ask the examinee to list the implications or conclusions from a statement, such as: A new invention makes it unnecessary for people to eat. What might be the consequences? Problems 2 and 3 in Figure 4.1 test for fluency.

By definition, the creative thinker produces *original* or novel ideas. This can be tested by counting the number of uncommon, yet acceptable, responses made to items on a word association test. A person who says "president" in association to "table" is scored as more original than one who says "chair," since few people produce the former response but many produce the latter. Another test involves asking for unusual uses for a common object, such as a brick or a clothes hanger. Problems 4 and 5 in Figure 4.1 can be scored for originality.

Creative thought is assumed to involve attacking a problem from a new direction, which implies *flexibility* of thought. One way to test this involves counting the frequency with which an examinee switches response categories when listing uses for a brick, for example (i. e., building material, weight, missile, and so on.) The flexible thinker switches categories frequently. Problem 5 in Figure 4.1 can be scored for flexibility.

Based on tests of these sorts, Guilford identified a large number of abilities contributing to human intellect. Those factors important to creativity involve two kinds of thinking ability, divergent thinking and convergent thinking, as well as an ability to evaluate information and draw conclusions. Sensitivity to problems is part of the evaluation ability. Equivalent to De Bono's notion of lateral thinking, divergent thinking requires fluency, flexibility, and originality to produce many different ideas in response to a problem. It is not ordinary logical thinking, but is more like free association and Freud's primary process thinking. Once many potential solutions are produced, convergent thinking determines whether any are useful. Brainstorming methods are designed to facilitate divergent thinking. In convergent thinking, on the other hand, one uses information to eliminate possibilities, as when one uses logic to deduce a single answer from various data.

To summarize, Guilford's work on creativity began with hypotheses concerning several traits which, on logical grounds, seemed to be important in creative thinking. Guilford and his colleagues developed tests to measure these traits. The resulting traits were combined into several factors or abilities, two of which, divergent and convergent thinking, are important in creativity.

Guilford's analysis is important for several reasons, one of which is that it provided a theoretic foundation for the creativity training being conducted in business and industry. Indeed, Guilford himself noted that his early hypotheses concerning creativity were received with strongest interest outside the psychological community.

As discussed, many theorists from diverse backgrounds have concluded that creativity involves an extraordinary type of thinking (i.e., divergent or lateral thinking) which depends on one's ability to respond to a problem with many ideas, some or most of which are atypical. In order to increase creative thinking, based on this view, thinkers must be taught to produce ideas that would not ordinarily occur in response to a particular problem.

Teaching Creativity

In order to give the reader a more concrete idea of how creative thinking is supposedly fostered, it is worthwhile to outline the events that might occur if one participated in a "typical" course designed to teach creative thinking. The contents of a well-known how-to book on creativity, James Adams's *Conceptual Blockbusting,* will serve as the primary source for discussion.

Many people believe that creativity cannot be taught, which obviously puts the author of a how-to-think-creatively book at a disadvantage. In order to convince readers that he has something of value to teach, Adams begins with an example of how one can improve one's golf game by becoming conscious of the various things involved in hitting the ball. In the same vein, Adams hopes to make the reader conscious of the various aspects of the creative process. He or she is first made aware of the various blocks that inhibit creative thinking in order to overcome them. Adams discusses four main types of blocks to creativity: perceptual, emotional, cultural and environmental, and intellectual and expressive blocks. He then presents various tricks that can augment the creative process. Once one has overcome the blocks to creativity, therefore, one will be able to increase one's output of creative ideas still further.

Blocks that Inhibit the Creative Process   Human perception is strongly influenced by what the perceiver expects to see, and these *perceptual expectations* can interfere with creative problem solving in various ways. Adams uses the nine-dot problem, which was discussed extensively in the preceding chapter, as an example of a perceptual block. In this problem, according to Adams, experience causes one to delimit the problem too closely; that is, one assumes that the square's boundaries cannot be crossed, thereby making it impossible to solve the problem (see Gestalt theory, Chapter 3).

Another example of a perceptual block occurs when one's past experience makes it difficult for one to look at a problem from various viewpoints. So long as one is locked within one viewpoint, producing the original ideas required to solve a difficult problem will be impossible. In this context, Adams refers to De Bono's distinction between vertical and lateral thinking. In vertical thinking, an old viewpoint is applied to the problem at hand, while in lateral thinking, a new viewpoint is achieved by a lateral or sideways move which can produce a novel solution to the problem. To use De Bono's analogy: vertical thinking involves making an old hole deeper, while lateral thinking involves digging a new hole. Sometimes, according to De Bono, to find treasure, you may have to dig a new hole. Again, Guilford's concept of divergent thinking captures the same idea.

A person's negative emotional response to a problem solving situation can interfere with their ability to explore and manipulate ideas. According to Adams, one *emotional block* to creative thinking is fear of taking a risk, since production of a creative idea involves taking risks. In order to help one overcome such blocks, Adams suggests that one try to assess the consequences realistically. What will *really* happen if one proposes an idea that others think is foolish and/ or does not work? Will one be held in less esteem? Adams hopes that such an assessment will make it clear that the *actual* consequences are not really that terrible, and convince one to risk trying to be creative.

One particularly important emotional block involves judging rather than generating ideas. Judging is safer than attempting to generate something new, and people often concentrate on judging ideas, to the exclusion of generating them. One particularly important difficulty can arise when one judges a newly formed idea too early and rejects it before all its implications are considered. A potentially useful idea may be rejected before the thinker realizes that it could solve his or her problem. The technique of brainstorming was developed explicitly to deal with the problem of premature use of judgment. Brainstorming has been particularly important in the creative teaching movement, and the latter part of this chapter will examine its effectiveness.

Adams believes that our culture's emphasis on logic and reasoning in thinking stifles creative thinking, which depends more on intuition, and he presents various methods for "thinking through" such *cultural blocks*. In addition to the cultural attitude as a whole, one's immediate environment can also produce blocks to creativity. For example, one may experience a lack of cooperation from one's co-workers, or one's environment may contain excessive distractions. These *environmental blocks* seem relatively easy to overcome, and Adams only briefly discusses them.

Intellectual blocks occur when a thinker is unable to approach a problem in the most efficient way. He or she may be inflexible in their use of problem solving strategies, or may not have adequate information before beginning the problem. *Expressive blocks* interfere with one's ability to communicate ideas during problem solving. The communication may be with others or with oneself, as when one tries to solve a problem verbally though use of mathematics would be more efficient.

To summarize, Adams presents a varied catalogue of difficulties, or blocks, which can arise when one tries to produce a creative solution to a problem. These blocks range from basic difficulties in human cognition (perceptual blocks) to difficulties arising from external distractions (environmental blocks). The next step in Adams's method is to present various ways to overcome these blocks.

Blockbusting   Adams discusses many different blockbusting methods that are proposed to help overcome the various blocks to creativity. He first considers methods that enable the thinker to produce thoughts he or she would not produce ordinarily. One general method of this sort is simply to have a questioning attitude, because it enables one to be sensitive to questions and "problems" that others never see. Furthermore, this attitude can be achieved by conscious effort; if one begins to ask questions, it soon becomes habitual. In order to increase fluency, or the production of ideas, Adams recommends making lists. These help one to concentrate on the problem at hand, making it easier to produce a larger number of ideas.

The second type of blockbusting method concerns "freeing the unconscious." Adams accepts the view that creative thinking depends on the unconscious, and that we sometimes are not creative because we are unable to give our unconscious free rein. Several different techniques are possible if one accepts this view. Adams suggests psychoanalysis as one possibility, although he realizes it is not a realistic goal for most people due to the time and expense involved. Another possibility involves the various esoteric psychologies of the Middle East that have evolved from Buddhism and Yoga. Though these practices presumably contain techniques for freeing the unconscious, practical problems again arise, due to the time and effort that learning these techniques demand.

One easier method for ordinary people to adopt involves education. Adams believes that learning about psychological processes can loosen the control of one's ego over the unconscious. Several additional methods have been developed to free one's thinking from conscious control, the most influential of which is brainstorming.

To summarize, courses in creative thinking are typically organized around the notion that all people are capable of thinking creatively if they are not blocked from doing so. The courses reveal the different sorts of blocks that supposedly occur and then provide methods for overcoming them.

Brainstorming

Most of the modern methods of improving creativity are directly based on, or are closely related to, the notion of brainstorming, which was elaborated by Alex Osborn in a series of books, speeches, and seminars. Osborn's books present his ideas with a patriotic fervor that seems very old-fashioned today, but in the 1950s it was hoped that increasing the creativity of American scientists and engineers would enable the United States to defeat the Russians in the cold war and keep the world safe for freedom.

Before considering the brainstorming method in detail, it is important to note that the term is used in two slightly different ways. Though one often hears the phrase "Let's brainstorm it," what is meant is "Let's get together and toss ideas around." The term also refers to something more technical, however, a specific set of rules to be used in order to foster creative thinking in groups of people. A discussion of this latter use of the term follows.

Osborn begins his analysis with the assumption that all people possess creative capacity. He divides the thinking mind into two components: *judicial mind,* which analyzes, compares, and chooses, and *creative mind,* which visualizes, foresees, and generates ideas. Although one is born with a creative capacity, this capacity can dwindle over the years as one becomes increasingly judgmental. Judgment, as discussed previously, can sometimes interfere with creativity.

One becomes more judgmental with age, according to Osborn, because most life situations involve judgment rather than creativity, encouraging this capacity to become stronger while the capacity for creativity wanes. Most importantly, *premature* judgment can interfere with creativity when it causes one to reject as incorrect ideas that might solve the problem if given the chance. In addition, judgment can interfere with creative problem solving when it appears in the form of habits that prevent one from approaching a problem in a new way.

The brainstorming technique is designed to offset the inhibiting effect of premature judgment and to make it possible for problem solvers to produce as many wild ideas as possible, in order to maximize the chance that a potentially useful idea is produced. Osborn emphasizes the value of "copious ideation" (that is, producing many ideas) in creative thinking. He presents examples of scientists and inventors whose creative accomplishments depended on an exhaustive examination of every hypothesis before finding the solution to the problem. One such example is Thomas Edison, who tested hundreds of different materials until he finally found one that could be used as a filament in a light bulb.

Four basic rules govern any brainstorming session.

1. Criticism is ruled out. Adverse judgment of ideas is withheld until later. No judgment is made of any idea until all ideas have been produced.

2. Freewheeling is welcomed. Because it is easier to tame down than to think up, the wilder the idea the better. An idea that is too wild may be modified in a way that solves the problem, but if it is never produced in the first place, nothing will be accomplished.

3. Quantity is wanted. The more ideas, the greater the likelihood of winners.

4. Combination and improvement are sought. In addition to contributing ideas of their own, participants suggest how the ideas of others can be made better, or how two or more ideas can be joined into still another idea. Different individuals have different sets of ideas, and one may see implications in the ideas of others that were not apparent to those who produced them. Therefore, a group may carry a given idea much further than an individual might. Furthermore, since a creative solution to a problem often involves old ideas in a new form, active encouragement of such combinations is important.

Examination of these rules makes apparent much of the philosophy behind brainstorming. According to Osborn, creative thinking depends upon the free flow of ideas. People have trouble thinking creatively because they tend to judge their own ideas, and those of others, too quickly. Such judgment stifles idea production. To help keep ideas flowing, the brainstorming rules actively prohibit such judgment. Second, to loosen inhibitions, the emphasis is on "wild" ideas. Third, the emphasis on *quantity*, not quality, is intended to loosen any inhibitions participants may have concerning whether an idea is good or not. Finally, to take advantage of the particular knowledge and experience of each individual in the group, the emphasis is on combination.

Although the rules are obviously very important, brainstorming groups are not made up of simple random collections of individuals asked to solve problems. Each brainstorming group must have a trained leader who structures the situation in such a way that the rules are used most effectively. Group leaders are instructed to foster a warm, supportive atmosphere to make group members feel free to report any ideas they may have, no matter how wild. Also, the leader encourages all members of the group to participate so that no one or two members dominate the group's thinking. Osborn emphasizes his own experiences in situations in which a quiet member of a group eventually produced the most valuable ideas after being encouraged to speak. In addition, the type of problem to be solved is an important factor in determining the effectiveness of brainstorming. The problem should be quite specific so group members have a precise goal to work toward. Rather than try to solve the problem of how to improve one's life, for example, it would be better to begin with the question of how one could make evenings with one's family more enjoyable.

To summarize, the brainstorming technique attempts to foster creativity by making it easier to produce many ideas. This is done by withholding judgment until many ideas have been produced, including those that might have seemed ridiculous initially. This restriction, combined with an active interchange of ideas by several people, seem reasonable steps to assure that a group will produce many novel and potentially valuable ideas—ideas that a single judgmental individual could not produce alone. These seemingly reasonable assumptions deserve examination.

Is Brainstorming Helpful?

Osborn presents varied evidence which he feels demonstrates brainstorming's remarkable success in generating useful ideas. He first points to the many organizations that have adopted the method to foster employee creativity—and the list reads like a who's-who of business, from Alcoa, DuPont, General Electric, and IBM, to RCA and US Steel. When brainstorming was used by the Advanced Development Section of the Television Division at RCA, for example, one session devoted to the improvement of television receivers produced 200 ideas.

In addition, Osborn notes that in many cases the method was adopted initially by one unit within a company, such as one department in one factory, and then spread, first within the factory and then to the entire company. Several institutes at universities have adopted the method in training creativity also, the most well-known of which is at the State University of New York at Buffalo, which has been attended by thousands of people since Osborn helped establish it over 20 years ago.

Brainstorming also was adopted by various branches of the United States government, and Osborn reports some impressive results concerning its effectiveness. In one 40-minute session, a group of U.S. Treasury personnel brainstormed the question of how to encourage federal employees to sell more U.S. Savings Bonds and produced 103 ideas. A group brainstorming the question of how to reduce absenteeism produced 89 ideas in 30 minutes. In a creative thinking course conducted by the Adjutant General School of the U.S. Army, a group brainstormed the question of how army recruiters could improve their techniques and produced 90 ideas in 12 minutes.

In summary, if one takes broad adoption as the basic criterion, then brainstorming seems very successful. If one also considers results Osborn reports, it seems without question that brainstorming is a highly effective technique for stimulating creative thinking.

From the point of view of a research-oriented psychologist, however, the case just presented for the effectiveness of brainstorming is not strong at all. The fact that a 20-member group brainstormed 72 ideas in 10 minutes about how to curb air pollution is impressive only if a comparable control group without brainstorming training produced *fewer* valuable ideas. Only controlled experiments can determine if the method is effective. Two groups of subjects must be chosen randomly and given the same or equivalent problems to solve, with one group instructed in brainstorming and the other given no such instructions, before one can draw direct conclusions concerning the importance of the instructions. All of Osborn's results, therefore, really say nothing about whether brainstorming is effective because the necessary control groups were not tested. All of the results he reports are based on single groups of individuals. From this point of view, the fact that many institutions enthusiastically adopted brainstorming means nothing more than that Osborn was able to convince people of brainstorming's effectiveness.

Controlled studies have attempted to determine whether or not brainstorming is an effective technique by considering the two components of the method separately. First, there is the question of the group versus the individual. Osborn emphasizes that brainstorming works better in groups because the diverse backgrounds of people in a group can lead to more unique ideas than an individual could produce. Second is the issue of withholding judgment. With group elaboration, according to Osborn, a seemingly irrelevant or incorrect idea can lead to a solution or elicit additional ideas that then lead to a solution.

A number of different measures of creative problem solving must be considered in analyzing the results of these studies. Though one could simply compare the number of ideas produced by the two groups working under different instructions, this is not a very interesting measure because one's interest is in increasing creativity. Measuring the potential usefulness of the ideas produced, on the other hand, would enable one to score the number of good ideas produced under various conditions. Finally, if one determined the percentage of good ideas produced in a given condition, one would know something about the efficiency of a particular problem-solving method. The method used to analyze the results of a given study sometimes has a large effect on how the study is to be interpreted.

Group versus Individual Performance   A number of important studies compared the performance of groups versus individuals on various problems when all used brainstorming. In one such study by Marvin Dunnette, John Campbell, and Kay Jastaad, forty-eight subjects solved problems in twelve groups of four members each, while forty-eight other individuals solved the problems alone. The individuals' responses later were randomly combined into twelve groups of four members each as if they had actually worked in a group. In this way, the results of the real groups could be compared with those of the "nominal" groups in order to determine if working in a group is helpful.

The Dunnette study tested two types of subjects: ninety-six research scientists and ninety-six workers in advertising. Each subject participated in both individual and group sessions, solving two problems in each situation. The problems were of comparable levels of difficulty. All participants used brainstorming. To minimize inhibitions, groups were selected so that the members were well-acquainted with one another.

Four problems were used in the study. In the *thumbs* problem, one was asked to anticipate the consequences that might arise if people were born with an extra thumb on each hand. The *education* problem asked subjects to determine what steps a school system might take to deal with a "bulge" in enrollment due to a baby boom. The *people* problem asked subjects to speculate on what might happen if the average size of humans increased to 80 inches and the average weight doubled. Finally, in the *tourists* problem, subjects were asked to suggest steps that would increase the number of European tourists visiting the United States.

The analysis of the results included the number of different ideas produced by a real or nominal group. If two or more members of a nominal group produced the same idea while working alone, that idea was counted only once when the responses were combined to make a nominal group. In addition to determining *number* of responses, independent judges rated the *quality* of each as a solution to the problem in question.

The results, which were consistent for each problem, indicate that working in groups is less effective than working alone. The nominal groups averaged 30–40 percent more solutions to each problem, and the quality of these solutions was consistently rated higher. These results, which clearly indicate that brainstorming in groups is not as effective as in individuals, raise a question about one of the basic assumptions underlying Osborn's program. In considering why the real groups performed worse than the individuals, Dunnette et al. noted that the groups tended to "fall into a rut" and pursue the same train of thought longer than individuals did. This is surprising, at first glance, since one of the reasons for advocating group problem solving is supposedly to allow one person to respond to the idea of another and thus carry the thinking process farther along than an individual could alone.

The Dunnette study also noted that some individuals were inhibited by being in a group. This is especially important, since this study attempted to place individuals who knew each other in the same group—that is, group members were as close as one might reasonably expect co-workers to be. Though this should have served to minimize inhibition, the results indicate that even at its minimum, inhibition remained significant.

One limitation of the Dunnette study is that group size remained constant at four, so that one cannot generalize beyond that. It is possible that with larger groups, the real groups might have performed better than the nominal groups. Thomas Bouchard and M. Hare's study comparing the performance of real and nominal groups made up of five, seven, and nine subjects working on the "thumbs" problem replicated the findings of Dunnette et al. The nominal groups outperformed the real groups at each size, and the difference between the two conditions *increased* as group size increased. In addition, a study by P. Dillon, W. Graham, and A. Aidells compared nominal versus real groups on a more complicated and engaging problem. The study was conducted soon after the United States first invaded Cambodia, and the question to be dealt with was how Americans could have more influence on their government's foreign policy. Here again, the nominal groups performed better than the real groups did.

In conclusion, these seems no doubt that one of the basic assumptions behind the advocacy of brainstorming is incorrect. Placing individuals in groups does not foster idea production, and the larger the group the greater the interference. It is interesting to note that Bouchard recently concluded that the difference in nominal and real groups was misinterpreted by workers in creativity. Group problem solving, he feels, cannot be abandoned because there are at least two situations when it is necessary for people to work in groups. The first is when the problem requires several different types of expertise, and the second is when one wants to maximize the chance that a solution will be accepted. (A group is more effective than an individual in convincing the directors of a company, for example, to adopt an innovative solution to a problem.)

Based on these results, if a problem involves several different kinds of specialized knowledge, it is probably advisable for individuals to work alone on the part of the problem requiring their expertise, and then pass the problem along to another individual when other expertise is needed. After the problem is solved, the individuals could jointly present the solution to the board of directors. Though the results of these controlled studies indicate that the brainstorming technique does not cause groups to perform better than individuals do, is brainstorming itself the best method for a problem solver to use?

Deferring Judgment versus Voicing Criticism   The second and more important assumption underlying Osborn's program is that brainstorming is the most effective method of problem solving, because by deferring judgment many ideas are elaborated that would otherwise be rejected before being considered. A number of experimental studies compared the performance of subjects given brainstorming instructions to that of subjects told to criticize their own ideas in various ways. The results of many of these studies raise difficulties for those who argue that deferring judgment is critical in creative problem solving.

Edith Weisskopf-Joelson and Thomas Eliseo compared the quantity and quality of ideas produced by groups of Purdue University undergraduates given two sorts of instructions. Some groups were given brainstorming instructions and others were given instructions that placed more emphasis on critical analysis as ideas were produced. These critical groups were told to think clearly and logically; to try and see all aspects of the problem; to produce as many ideas as possible; but to make them good, practical ideas; and, finally, to combine and improve the ideas discussed. The groups were given the problem of inventing brand names for a cigarette, a deodorant, and an automobile designed for Purdue students. Ten minutes were given for each task. The brand names produced by the groups were then rated on a five-point quality scale by another group of 150 Purdue students.

The results revealed that the brainstorming groups produced more ideas overall, but not more good ideas. The critical groups produced fewer ideas overall, but the same number of high-quality ideas as the brainstorming groups produced. On the average, therefore, the critical groups produced better ideas and a higher proportion of high-quality ideas as well. Contrary to the critical assumption of the brainstorming procedure, this study indicates that giving groups some criteria to use during idea production increases the average quality of ideas by eliminating some bad ideas.

This conclusion is supported by the results of a study by John Brilhart and Lurene Jochem, who gave three different sorts of instructions to different groups of subjects who then worked on the tourist and education problems and a third problem of a similar sort. Some groups were given standard brainstorming instructions, emphasizing idea production followed by evaluation. The second type of instructions reversed the usual brainstorming procedure by telling subjects first to set criteria for generating solutions, that is, to decide what standards to use to assess solutions, and then to use brainstorming. Thus, these two sets of groups both used brainstorming, but the use of criteria differed. Brainstorming was not used at all in the final set of groups. These *criteria* groups were given the following criteria for analyzing the problem and evaluating solutions. 1) What is the problem? What is happening? Why? How serious is it? 2) How should we solve it? What are the relative merits of the ideas we can think of? 3) What do we report as the best solution? These instructions emphasize judgment and make no mention of brainstorming. Subjects were given 35 minutes for each problem, and solutions were rated for quality.

The results of the study, presented in Table 4.1, bear some analysis because they raise interesting questions of interpretation. As can be seen, the groups whose instructions involved brainstorming produced more ideas than the criteria group. The figures in the second column of the table imply that the two groups using brainstorming also performed better, that is, they produced more

Table 4.1
Results of brainstorming study.

Instructions to subjects	Total ideas produced	Good ideas produced	% good ideas
Standard brainstorming (ideas, then criteria for evaluation)	15.1	4.37	29
Reversed brainstorming	15.0	3.67	24
Criteria alone	9.8	3.11	32

good ideas overall. Based on their analysis of these results, Brilhart and Jochem concluded that it was necessary to use brainstorming, though it did not matter whether you used criteria before or after brainstorming. In the last column of the table, however, I have calculated the *percentage* of good ideas produced by each group. As can be seen, although the criteria group produced the fewest ideas overall, they produced the largest percentage of good ideas. Thus, the results in Table 4.1 do not support the idea that brainstorming is crucial for effective performance, since the criteria group performed more efficiently.

While we can now assume that criteria do not necessarily interfere with good idea production, the results discussed so far are still somewhat inconclusive. A supporter of brainstorming could argue that the results in Table 4.1 show that brainstorming produces *more* good ideas. Though problem solvers will work harder overall, they will produce more good ideas along with more bad ideas. If one is interested only in the absolute number of good ideas, brainstorming still seems to be the method of choice. Even this weaker claim for brainstorming was shown to be false, however, by the results of several additional experiments. Vernon Gerlach, Richard Schutz, Robert Baker, and Gilbert Mazer used four different types of instructions, including brainstorming and what they called "criteria-cued" instructions, in which subjects were told how their responses would be evaluated for "creativeness." The criteria-cued subjects produced fewer responses overall and the largest number of superior responses. Similar results were reported by Donald Johnson, George Parrott, and R. Paul Stratton, who told subjects beforehand what the criteria for a good solution were for five different sorts of problems. Criteria-cued subjects again produced fewer solutions overall, but produced more high-quality solutions.

To summarize, evidence strongly contradicts the claim that withholding judgment is important for creative thinking and, in fact, supports the opposite. In other words, the more one knows about the criteria a solution must meet, and the greater role these criteria play in the actual generation of solutions, the better the solution will be. Thus, if one wishes to solve a problem effectively, one should try to determine as precisely as possible what criteria the solution must meet before starting work on the problem, try to keep these criteria in mind as one works, and work alone.

Why Brainstorming Does Not Work

If one makes certain assumptions about creative thinking, brainstorming seems to be a plausible method for fostering creativity. These assumptions are first, that creative solutions to problems occur when one can approach them from a fresh point of view (the notion that "divergent thinking" is important in creativity); second, that many wild ideas are needed to obtain this viewpoint; and third, that most people fail to produce wild ideas because they are too judgmental initially. Based on these assumptions, if one could reduce or eliminate early judgment of ideas, one should foster creativity.

The research findings just reviewed indicate rather conclusively that brainstorming is not an effective method of increasing creative thinking. Therefore, one or more of these assumptions is wrong. Two of these assumptions are worth reconsidering here, in order to learn something more about what factors *are* involved in creative thinking.

Perhaps the most important assumption supporting the belief in brainstorming is the notion that divergent thinking is crucial in creativity. However, there is much evidence to indicate that this is not correct. First, consider again the results from the experiments discussed in Chapter 1 involving the candle and Charlie problems. Subjects produce creative solutions to both problems, but detailed analysis of various experimental data provides no evidence of anything like divergent thinking occurring. That is, at no time do people sit back and attempt to free associate, or anything like it, to elements in the problem. The ideas produced are relatively directly based on what the person is trying to do and what he or she knows about the objects in the problem situation. In the Charlie problem, for example, the realization that Charlie is not a human being is not achieved as the result of some sort of free-associative or divergent thinking process, rather it comes about when the problem solver acquires the information that makes Charlie's human status unlikely or impossible. In the same way, using the box as a candle holder to solve the candle problem also evolves as the individual works through the problem. Thus, creative solutions to problems do not involve divergent thinking, but come about by means of thought processes that are no different from these involved in other sorts of thinking. Similar results have been reported with other types of laboratory problems.

In addition, divergent thinking does not appear to be involved in creative scientific thinking either, indicating that its absence in laboratory problems is not due to some peculiar aspect of those problems. Two types of evidence imply that divergent thinking is unimportant in science. First, a number of detailed reports of scientific discovery are available, including Charles Darwin's notebooks concerning the development of the theory of evolution by natural selection, and James Watson's report of the discovery of the structure of the DNA molecule. These two examples are covered in detail in a later chapter, where it is shown that nothing like divergent thinking occurred in either discovery. Second, a number of studies examined the relationship between divergent thinking and scientific creativity by giving divergent thinking test to scientists of different degrees of creativity. In these studies, it was uniformly shown that performance on divergent thinking tests was unrelated to scientific creativity, as judged by other scientists in the same field. That is, the most creative scientists do not perform best on tasks involving divergent thinking, and those who perform better on the divergent thinking tests are not the most creative in their profession. Thus, divergent thinking tests do not measure those factors involved in scientific creativity.

In summary, one of the assumptions that interest in brainstorming grew from is that divergent thinking is important in creativity, but studies of several sorts indicate that this assumption is incorrect.

A second important assumption underlying the interest in methods of fostering divergent thinking is that creative solutions involve approaching the problem from a fresh viewpoint. The creative person, it assumes, is somehow able to break away from past experience (vertical thinking) to a new way of looking at the problem (divergent thinking). This assumption seems so obviously true that it hardly needs any discussion, but I believe it is based on a mistaken analysis by theorists of how other people solve a problem. To make this clear, consider an alleged example of divergent thinking discussed by De Bono.

> For many years physiologists could not understand the purpose of the long loops in the kidney tubules: it was assumed that the loops had no special function and were a relic of the way the kidney had evolved. Then one day an engineer looked at the loops and at once recognized that they could be part of a counter-current multiplier, a well-known engineering device for increasing the concentration of solutions. In this instance, a fresh look from outside provided an answer to something that had been a puzzle for a long time.

In this example, the engineer's knowledge provided a fresh way of seeing things and thus solved the physiologists' puzzle. In other words, when one is trying to solve a difficult problem, one should try to generate a fresh way of looking at it. If the physiologist had been able to think divergently, he or she could have solved the puzzle of the loops in the kidney tubules. However, there is a mistaken analogy here between what the engineer did and what a "divergent thinking" physiologist could have done. From the point of view of the *physiologist,* the engineer clearly brought a fresh viewpoint to the problem; from the point of view of the *engineer,* on the other hand, a fresh viewpoint was not involved. The engineer simply applied old knowledge to a new situation and recognized its similarity to something already known.

Summary

This chapter focused on the brainstorming method of increasing creativity in order to critically analyze the view that creative thinking depends primarily on divergent or lateral thinking. Unlike logical thinking, this sort of thinking is assumed to occur when a thinker overcomes blocks and allows the associational process (some of which may be unconscious) free rein. The method of brainstorming was developed to facilitate this "free-form" thinking by eliminating judgment of ideas and by having groups of people work together so that they can build on each other's ideas. The results discussed in this chapter, however, question both the usefulness of brainstorming and the assumptions underlying the belief in it, particularly the assumption that creativity depends on divergent or lateral thinking.

Research indicates that both of the crucial assumptions behind the brainstorming technique are incorrect: group problem solving is less productive than that of individuals, and brainstorming instructions are less effective than instructions that emphasize initial criteria and judgment. Second, studies also indicate that creative scientific thinking is not related to divergent thinking ability. Finally, an examination of the logic in the notion of divergent thinking concludes that a basic misunderstanding may be involved in the development of that concept. Though someone else may solve a problem from what you consider a "fresh viewpoint," it does not mean the viewpoint was fresh from *their* point of view. If so, then trying to make oneself find that fresh point of view may be essentially impossible because it really means that one must transform oneself into another person, with that person's knowledge, before one can bring a new approach to a problem. But then the viewpoint would not be fresh because one had acquired all that knowledge.

In conclusion, this chapter provides further evidence that creative thinking is not an extraordinary form of thinking. Creative thinking becomes extraordinary because of what the thinker produces, not because of the *way* in which the thinker produces it. This conclusion is further supported when the thought processes of creative individuals in science and in the arts are considered in later chapters.

5

THE MYTH OF GENIUS

We have discussed creative *acts* and the thought process involved in them, that is whether such acts occur through leaps of imagination and whether they involve unconscious thought processes. Another, different stream of research has attempted to specify the characteristics of creative *individuals*. This research investigated such questions as how the personality characteristics of creative individuals differ from those of the population as a whole, and what factors influence the development of such characteristics. Western thinkers have been interested in what these differences might be for a long time. Some possible differences have already been discussed, such as the idea that creative genius involves inspiration from the gods and that the source of creative genius is madness. Both views date back at least to the ancient Greeks, and both are to be found in present-day theorizing about creativity. The work considered in this chapter is based on much less exotic notions, though it too can be traced back to those early attempts to answer the question of what made the creative person different from ordinary individuals.

The first part of this chapter briefly reviews current knowledge concerning the psychological characteristics assumed to be the basis for creative genius in the sciences and the arts. This research sought to isolate the characteristics of creative individuals by giving them personality tests. The remainder of the chapter raises several questions about this research. Specifically, it examines the study designs used, looks at the concept of genius, and asks what "being a genius" entails. These analyses raise the possibility that the search for genius is misdirected and that the concept of genius, defined as psychological characteristics of a creative individual, is a myth.

The research results discussed here are taken from studies that measured the personality characteristics of individuals of varying degrees of creativity. In order to get a clear idea of exactly what is involved in measuring personality, Figure 5.1 presents examples of several instruments used by personality psychologists.

The Study of Values test measures six traits individuals are assumed to possess to varying degrees. These values are assumed to be beliefs that help direct people's behavior and structure their lives. The six measured values are: theoretical (interest in truth); economic (interest in things for their usefulness); esthetic (a search for harmony); social (altruistic love); political (power); and religious (belief in an all-encompassing unity). Based on responses to such items one can determine how firmly an individual holds various values. One can also compare

A.

Which of the following branches of study do you expect ultimately will prove more important for mankind? (*a*) mathematics; (*b*) theology.

Which would you consider the more important function of modern leaders? (*a*) to bring about the accomplishment of practical goals; (*b*) to encourage followers to take a greater interest in the rights of others.

When witnessing a gorgeous ceremony (ecclesiastical or academic, induction into office, etc.), are you more impressed: (*a*) by the color and pageantry of the occasion itself; (*b*) by the influence and strength of the group?

Which of the following would you prefer to do during part of your next summer vacation (if your ability and other conditions would permit)—
a. write and publish an original biological essay or article
b. stay in some secluded part of the country where you can appreciate fine scenery
c. enter a local tennis or other athletic tournament
d. get experience in some new line of business

Do great exploits and adventures of discovery, such as Columbus's, Magellan's, Byrd's, and Amundsen's, seem to you significant because—
a. they represent conquests by man over the difficult forces of nature
b. they add to our knowledge of geography, meteorology, oceanography, etc.
c. they weld human interests and international feelings throughout the world
d. they contribute each in a small way to an ultimate understanding of the universe

B.

Do you agree or disagree?
    Sometimes I think I may kill myself.
    My greatest troubles are inside myself.
    I certainly have little self-assurance.
    I wish I were not so awkward.
    I am shy.

Fig. 5.1

A. Values questionnaire. B. Items superior to those on the MMPI. (Sample items from G. W. Allport, P. E. Vernon, and G. Lindzey, 1960, *A Study of Values,* Boston, Houghton Mifflin.)

the strengths of an individual's values with those of various groups for which normative data are available.

Several personality inventories are used to assess personality characteristics, but the most influential is the Minnesota Multiphasic Personality Inventory (MMPI). Personality inventories are long questionnaires in which respondents are usually asked to respond to general statements about themselves rather than to respond to concrete situations. The questions in Figure 5.1 are similar to items on the MMPI. An individual's responses to the MMPI items are analyzed by grouping them together into a small number of scales, each of which contains items that are related to other measures of behavior (such as psychiatrists' diagnoses). Some of the scales of the MMPI are paranoia, depression, social introversion, and masculinity-femininity. An individual's scores on these various scales provide a profile of his or her personality. Many other questionnaires have evolved out of the MMPI, such as the California Personality Inventory, and the Taylor Manifest Anxiety Scale.

Research comparing personality and other psychological characteristics of creative versus noncreative individuals attempts to isolate the characteristics that make up genius. In addition, it is assumed that such characteristics may be present in varying degrees of strength in individuals. One can learn something about genius, therefore, by studying a sample of successful physicists, though none have the stature of Albert Einstein or Isaac Newton. Although questions can be raised about this assumption, I shall assume it is true.

There are several reasons why the characteristics of genius continue to interest students of creativity.

First, if the personal characteristics common to all creative individuals could be isolated, one could determine which individuals possess the potential for creative work. One could measure this potential in children, for example, by giving them personality tests. Those who most strongly showed the characteristics of genius could be placed in special educational programs that fully stimulated their creative potential.

Second, if one knew what characteristics creative adults possessed, one could increase creativity in other individuals by instilling those characteristics in them through education.

Finally, if one could isolate the personal characteristics of creative individuals, and also determine the child-rearing practices that brought them about, one could then teach parents methods of child rearing that maximized the chances of these characteristics occurring.

Thus, the discovery of a few characteristics common to all creative individuals would enable us to increase creativity in the population as a whole. This, presumably, would greatly increase our chances of solving the many problems that plague modern civilization.

It is interesting to compare this point of view about increasing creativity with the methods of teaching creative thinking discussed in Chapter 4. The courses designed to increase creative thinking, through brainstorming, etc., are based on the assumption all people are capable of creative thinking, if they only knew the methods. Creative thinking is considered a skill that can be taught to just about everyone. The viewpoint just discussed, on the other hand, conceives of creative individuals as basically different from the rest of the population by their possession of certain crucial psychological traits. In order to make a noncreative person capable of thinking creatively, therefore, one must change those crucial aspects of his or her personality. Creative thinking is not a simple skill that anyone can learn, but rather one expression of the whole individual. In order to make a person creative, one must change the person.

Before one can assess the characteristics of creative individuals, one must be able to identify such individuals, and the criteria for such identification have raised some problems in the literature. In some cases, especially in studies of children, creativity has been defined on the basis of scores on "creativity tests." As discussed in Chapter 4, however, the divergent thinking abilities which such tests measure are not related to "real world" creativity, since successful scientists and artists do not necessarily score highly on such tests. Because of such difficulties with creativity tests, the discussion here is based on studies of individuals whose creativity was determined by other means. In each case, the criteria for classifying individuals as creative are specified.

Some Characteristics of Genius

This section presents a distillation of the research exploring the personality characteristics of creative individuals in various domains. It is generally believed that comparisons of creative and noncreative individuals have yielded a small number of characteristics all creative individuals share. Among these are broad interests, independence of judgment, self-confidence, intuition, and a firm sense of the self as "creative." Such characteristics are reasonably straightforward and most need little further discussion. Intuition, however, refers to the tendency to reach a conclusion or carry out an action without explicitly reasoning through each step in the process. It presumably involves making "leaps," rather than taking precise steps. A firm sense of the self as creative means exactly that—creative individuals tend to believe they are creative, and this belief is a strong motivator of their work. That is, they work in an area at least in part because they believe they are capable of doing creative work in it.

In addition to these common core characteristics, some critical differences are thought to exist between creative individuals in the sciences and in the arts.

Creative scientists are believed to be different from noncreative scientists by their need to be free of rules (flexibility), and their ability to be more open to experience. This latter characteristic is particularly important because it is assumed that openness to experience makes the creative scientist more *sensitive to problems* than his or her noncreative colleague is. One difference between creative and noncreative scientists is that creative scientists are more sensitive to important research problems; that is, the creative scientist somehow knows which sorts of problems to concentrate on. Possessing scientific genius involves the ability to sense where significant scientific breakthroughs can be made. Those with genius do not waste time and effort on problems that are either impossible to solve or so simple that solving them has no significant effect. In addition, in some cases a scientist of genius may see a problem where no one else does, resulting in the creation of an original area of research.

The importance of such sensitivity to problems was hypothesized by J. P. Guilford in his presidential address to the American Psychological Association (see Chapter 4). Sensitivity to problems is supposedly measured by several tests of divergent thinking (see Chapter 4) in which one is asked, for example, to predict the consequences of humans suddenly developing an extra finger. Individuals who are more sensitive to problems, and are therefore more creative, presumably, would be able to infer many more consequences from a given event than would noncreative individuals.

Sensitivity to problems is often emphasized in accounts of the exploits of famous scientists, as in this comment on Lord Rutherford, a Nobel Prize winning physicist.

> In physics radioactivity had become the fashion, just as later on the atom would be, and then the nucleus. And in every case, Rutherford was in at the start: he had chosen just the right problem to study at the right time.

The importance of this sensitivity is also seen in Einstein's much-quoted statement that the really creative act in science involves initially forming the correct questions, rather than providing the answers.

In addition to knowing what sorts of problems to work on, the scientist of genius knows when to quit and when to adopt a better approach to a problem. The creative scientist is more likely to know when work is without benefit now —and in the future—and should be abandoned. This ability is assumed to be due to his or her openness to experience. In his investigation of the skills of chess masters, Adrian deGroot found similar evidence: masters waste no time contemplating worthless moves, but poor players waste a great deal. To take an analogy from deGroot, the scientist of genius is like the chess master, and somehow knows how to reject the worthless ways of trying to solve some scientific problem.

In addition, because the creative scientist can change his or her approach to a problem (or to abandon it altogether) more easily than those who are not creative, their thought processes must be more flexible, less "stuck in ruts," than are those of noncreative scientists.

Artistic genius includes the ability to move others emotionally through one's work. It seems reasonable to assume that those who can do this are more sensitive and open to feelings. That is, artistic genius involves being attuned to the feelings of those who will be exposed to the work, which may also mean that one is more open to one's own emotional experience. This intuition concerning the audience's perception enables the artist of genius to strike an emotional chord in the audience; because the less creative artist is insensitive to the emotional responsiveness of the audience, his or her works appear to have no feeling.

In summary, it seems to be generally agreed that the characteristics of genius have been isolated. As Frank Barron and David M. Harrington comment in a review of the literature, the research brought no surprises, in that the findings correspond to the general beliefs our society has concerning the characteristics of creative scientists and artists. I, on the contrary, shall attempt to support the claim that very little has been learned about the characteristics of creative genius and, furthermore, that they cannot be isolated because the very concept of genius is in reality a myth.

Assumptions Concerning Genius

In order to critically analyze the notion of genius, it is first necessary to discuss several critical assumptions that lie behind the search for creative genius. Doubts concerning the validity of these assumptions raise additional questions about what is actually known about creative genius.

The first assumption underlying the search for genius is that creative individuals possess a set of characteristics that are not present to the same degree in the noncreative. It is first necessary to compare creative and noncreative individuals in a particular field to determine whether creative individuals do in fact consistently differ from the noncreatives. The characteristics just discussed come from such studies, but I hope to show that many of these studies are invalid.

It also is assumed that these personal characteristics, i.e., flexibility of thought, are *causally* related to creativity. That is, flexibility of thought is assumed somehow to play a role in the individual's creativity. The simple fact that creative individuals exhibit flexibility of thought, however, does not mean that the flexibility of thought causes them to be creative. Such flexibility of thought might be the result of being creative, rather than its cause. Thus, one must be cautious about inferring causality without direct evidence of it.

The third assumption is that "being creative," or "possessing genius," is a permanent characteristic throughout an individual's life. That is, if a creative individual were not consistently creative, at least within his or her chosen field, then the search for genius would be doomed to failure because there would essentially be no such thing as genius.

These assumptions are made explicit in the following quote from Frank Barron, one of the leaders in the attempt to specify the characteristics of genius.

> There is good reason for believing . . . that originality is almost habitual with persons who produce a really singular insight. The biography of the inventive genius commonly records a lifetime of original thinking, though only a few ideas survive and are remembered to fame. Voluminous productivity is the rule and not the exception among individuals who have made some noteworthy contribution. Original responses, it would seem, recur regularly in some persons, while there are other individuals who never depart from the stereotyped and the conventional in their thinking.
>
> If, then, some persons are regularly original, whereas others are regularly unoriginal, it must be the case that certain patterns of relatively enduring traits either facilitate or impede the production of original acts.

Thus, the beliefs explicitly stated are that a regular pattern of characteristics or traits is present in creative versus noncreative individuals, that these traits are causally related to an individual's being creative, and that genius is a constant characteristic of creative individuals.

The search for the psychological components of genius is based on one final, obvious assumption. It is assumed that genius is a psychological characteristic of an individual, or a set of such characteristics, much like having an I.Q. of 115, for example, or being a hypochondriac. Given this assumption, it is reasonable to attempt to measure the characteristics comprising genius, as one would measure any other psychological characteristic. Though this assumption seems so reasonable that it is absurd to even raise it, I hope to show that "possessing creative genius" is not a psychological characteristic, or set of characteristics, of an individual and cannot be assessed as if it were one's I.Q.

The discussion that follows examines each of these four assumptions: whether creative individuals possess a set of unique characteristics, whether such factors have a casual role, whether genius remains constant throughout the lives of great scientists and artists, and whether genius is simply a psychological characteristic of certain individuals. This discussion, I believe, will result in a very different understanding of what possessing genius entails. As before, my aim is to raise questions about these assumptions, not prove conclusively that they are incorrect. The critiques that follow, therefore, are not meant to be exhaustive, but merely suggestive.

Characteristics of Genius: The Crucial Comparison Group

In order to test the hypothesis that the creativity of individuals in a particular field is due their possession of a unique set of characteristics, it is crucial to choose a relevant comparison group. If we compared the personality characteristics of creative mathematicians with those of the general population, for example, any differences could be related to either or both of two factors: creativity versus lack of creativity or a career in mathematics versus no career in mathematics. That is, the general population differs from creative mathematicians in at least two ways, either of which could produce any differences found. In order to make conclusions concerning the personality characteristics underlying genius in mathematics, one must compare creative mathematicians with noncreative mathematicians. Furthermore, the noncreative mathematicians should preferably be as similar as possible to the creative mathematicians in other ways, such as work experience. Though the need for such a comparison group seems obvious, many studies in this area fail to include them, forcing one to question their conclusions. Many of the characteristics listed previously, in fact, came from invalid studies. Furthermore, Donald Mackinnon's study, which contains the best match between creative and comparison groups, produced negative results, although it is rarely interpreted in this way. Mackinnon's study usually is interpreted as proof of the difference between creative and noncreative individuals as regards certain specific psychological characteristics. As will be demonstrated shortly, however, the results actually show just the opposite.

Mackinnon's study examined the personality characteristics of forty of the most creative architects in the United States, as nominated by a panel of professors of architecture. The findings from this sample of unquestioned creativity were compared with those from two comparison groups. One of the control groups, chosen from the 1955 *Directory of Architects,* was simply matched with the creative group by age and location of practice, while the members of the second control group had also worked with one of the architects in the creative group for at least two years. Several measures of creativity and eminence in architecture, as computed by Mackinnon, indicated clear differences among the three groups. The associates of the creative architects fell between the two other groups in measures of creativity, but were much closer to the noncreative comparison group than to the creative group.

Given the differences in creativity, Mackinnon then compared several personality characteristics in the three groups. A very interesting pattern of responses emerged. The creative architects were significantly different from the noncreative comparison group on many of the personality scales. On the Study of Values (see Table 5.1), for example, the creative group scored much lower on the economic scale and much higher on the aesthetic scale. On the MMPI, the creative architects scored more feminine than the noncreative comparison group, which is evidence for a sensitivity to feelings and emotions, especially one's own. On thirteen of the eighteen scales of the California Psychological Inventory, the creative group's scores were significantly different from the noncreative group's. Overall, the creative group was less social, more sensitive, and less self-controlled, among other things.

On the whole, these findings would seem to be the basis for claims about the personality characteristics underlying genius in architecture, except for one complication: the comparatively noncreative architectual associates were remarkably similar to the creative group on all the measures mentioned above. Indeed, out of nearly forty scales on the three instruments just discussed, the creative group differed from their associates on only one—they scored lower on the economic scale on the Study of Values. Thus, the large differences in creativity and eminence, i.e., genius, between these groups were not accompanied by comparable differences in personality characteristics. Furthermore, it must be repeated that the forty creative architects in this study were among the most creative in the country, which means that the similar personality scores were not due to a lack of real differences in creativity between the creative group and their associates. The creative group were architects at the very top of their profession.

In summary, this study of the personality characteristics of architects of differing levels of creativity indicates that essentially no unique personality characteristics are related to genius in architecture. Mackinnon's results imply that there are no personality characteristics which, if instilled in an individual, would lead him or her to exhibit genius in architecture. To the degree that this conclusion has broader relevance, it raises grave doubts that there is "creative genius" to be found. Although this conclusion is based on analysis of only one study, it should be emphasized again that it is a particularly important study. It is often cited in the literature, though the lack of differences between the creative architects and their associates usually is mentioned only briefly or ignored altogether. In addition, the associates of the creative architects comprise a particularly well-matched comparison group. Because this study may be the most well-designed on the subject, the lack of differences between these two groups is extremely important.

Correlation versus Causation

Even if we ignore the negative results from MacKinnon's study of architects, there are still questions to be raised about the assumption that possession of certain personal characteristics is a cause of one's being or becoming a creative individual. Close examination of the literature reveals essentially no support for this assumption at present, because almost all of the studies of personality characteristics examine individuals who are already successful. A study might compare the personality characteristics of creative research scientists, for example, with those of a matched noncreative group. Differences in personality characteristics are then assumed to be the basis for differences in creativity between the two groups. That is, if the creative scientists are more autonomous than the noncreative group, it is then concluded that the autonomy contributed to their creativity. Such a conclusion is unjustified, however—all that has been demonstrated is a correlation between autonomy and creativity, not that the former was a cause of the latter.

Based only on the above hypothetical results, several conclusions are possible. Being autonomous may make one creative because one has a greater chance of going off on one's own while working on a problem, and this might increase the chances of one's coming up with a novel solution. On the other hand, the exact opposite might also be true—being creative might make one autonomous. Once successful in one's creative work, for example, one is more likely to have confidence in one's own way of doing things and not want to follow rules set down by others. As this hypothetical example shows, the fact that a correlation exists between two measures says nothing about which is the cause of which. To make matters even worse, it might also be true that there is no relationship between autonomy and creativity, even though the two are correlated. For example, it is sometimes found that more creative individuals come from better economic backgrounds than do less creative individuals. If so, being economically well-off may be the cause of both creativity and autonomy. In this way, creativity and autonomy might be completely unrelated, though correlated.

A correlation, therefore, reveals nothing about cause. In order to demonstrate that personality characteristics play a part in causing creativity, one must first assess the personalities of individuals who have not yet demonstrated creativity. One can then examine the relationship between various characteristics and *later* creativity. Positive results would then be the first step in establishing certain personality characteristics as crucial to the development of creativity.

Such an investigation was conducted by Jacob Getzels and Mihalyi Csikszentmihalyi who followed a group of artists from their art-student years through the beginnings of their careers. A total of 205 students, 94 men and 111 women, at the School of the Art Institute of Chicago were tested during their second or third year in the Institute's three-year program. Students were enrolled in one of four areas of specialization offered by the school: fine art, art education, advertising art, and industrial art. In addition, of the thirty-four male fine art majors, thirty-one were contacted seven years later, approximately five years after graduation, when they had had a chance to establish their careers. This later contact allowed the investigators to examine the relationship between personal characteristics, assessed in art school, and early success or lack of it in a fine arts career.

The art students differed from the general college population in some specific ways but not in others. On conventional measures of intelligence, for example, the art students as a group scored close to college norms. On two tests of perceptual abilities, however, they scored far above college norms, indicating that they possessed a specific set of strong skills. (These skills were probably important in enabling them to gain admission to a prestigious art school in the first place.)

When the personal characteristics were assessed, the art students as a whole showed certain differences when compared with general student norms. In addition, although the pattern of characteristics generally was similar for the four groups of art students, the fine arts majors tended to have the most extreme scores on the various scales, the advertising and industrial artists scored closest to the college norms, and art education majors scored in between. On the Study of Values, the art students as a whole scored extremely high on the aesthetic scale, apparently indicating strong commitment to their chosen careers. They also scored very low on the economic and social scales, indicating that the commitment to art as a career was not an unrealistic choice, since it is notoriously insecure financially and involves intense work, often with an accompanying sacrifice of social relationships.

On the Sixteen Personality Factors Questionnaire (16 PF), a questionnaire measuring various aspects of personality, the following composite portrait emerged when the art students were compared with college norms. Art students are socially aloof, introspective, self-sufficient, nonconforming to society's norms, radical, and experimental. They are also subjective and imaginative rather than conventional in their outlook. This pattern corresponds reasonably well to the popular stereotype of the artist.

As mentioned earlier, Getzels and Csikszentmihalyi's work is particularly important because they located thirty-one of these students seven years later, when they had been out of school five or six years. Although this length of time is obviously too short to determine which students, if any, would become artists of lasting reputation, large differences in success had already been achieved. Success was defined by two art experts and by the students' judgments of each other. This follow-up study enabled Getzels and Csikszentmihalyi to examine the relationship between career success and scores obtained on various measures when the men were students. Their findings are particularly relevant to the question of whether success in a fine arts career can be predicted from one's characteristics as a student, and whether any personality characteristics are causally related to creativity in fine art.

Of these thirty-one students, fifteen had severed all connections with the art world and would probably never make a significant contribution to it. Seven men were in careers only peripherally related to art, such as art teachers and model builders for architects. While some might later decide to go into art full-time, at the time of assessment they were obviously less successful than the remaining nine artists, who had succeeded in establishing places for themselves in the art world. Though most showed their work only sporadically, one artist had already achieved unqualified success.

Given the range of career success, Getzels and Csikszentmihalyi then examined the relationship between success and scores obtained on the various measures seven years before. The results are important in the present context because they reveal that essentially *none* of the measures obtained in art school related to career success. First, no standardized test of intelligence, cognition, or divergent thinking related to later success. The successful artists were not more intelligent and had not performed better on the divergent thinking tests in art school. The same was also true of the students' values—none of the scores on the Study of Values obtained in art school related to later success. The successful artists did not score significantly higher than the unsuccessful ones in the aesthetic value nor significantly lower in the economic and social values. Finally, the personality characteristics were little better as predictors of success. Only one of the 16 PF factors was significantly related to career success: the successful artists scored lower on the scale measuring conformity and concern with social approval. Given the sixteen factors involved, however, a significant difference on a single factor could very well be due to chance. In any case, no complex of factors were related in any direct way to later success.

To summarize, this study provides evidence that one cannot predict artistic success on the basis of characteristics measured earlier in the individual's life (or at least on the basis of those characteristics measured by Getzels and Csikszentmihalyi). Furthermore, it is important to emphasize that the investigators measured a relatively wide range of characteristics and found a reasonably wide range of success among the former students. One might conclude, therefore, that if any strong relationships existed, this study had a good chance of finding them. In conclusion, the results of this study support the research discussed in the last section in indicating that the search for the characteristics of genius may be misdirected.

Is Scientific Genius Constant?

The last section raised doubts about how to interpret the many studies that measured personality characteristics of creative individuals. Even if one assumes there is a causal relationship between certain personality traits and creativity, a problem remains which stems from the assumption that genius is a permanent characteristic of an individual. For the sake of ease of exposition, scientific genius and artistic genius will be discussed separately although, as will be seen, there are strong parallels between them.

One characteristic believed to be associated with scientific genius is a greater sensitivity to potentially solvable problems. The nongenius, on the other hand, may waste time on problems that have no solution. Studies of the lives of great scientists, however, provide much evidence that this assumption is incorrect. Many great scientists spent significant portions of their careers working in areas that produced no contribution of any value.

One example of such misdirection is seen in the career of Isaac Newton, one of the most creative scientists who ever lived. In addition to developing the laws that bear his name, producing seminal work on light, and inventing the calculus, Newton also spent twenty-five years in the study of alchemy, searching in secret for mysterious elixirs and forces to influence nature. This alchemical work led to no outcome of value, although Newton spent much time and wrote thousands of pages on it.

Another example of misdirected scientific genius is seen in the case of Alfred Russell Wallace who, independently of Charles Darwin, developed the theory of evolution through natural selection. Wallace's letter to Darwin stimulated Darwin to present his own ideas in public, along with those of Wallace. Later in his life, Wallace became interested in communicating with the dead and attempted to prove that "messages from the dead" were communications from spirits and not the work of fraudulent mediums. He also published papers claiming that the spirit world had helped bring about the rapid evolution of humans from apes.

Still another example of misdirected genius is found in the case of Franz Joseph Gall, one of the pioneers in the study of the structure of the brain. On the basis of his dissections, Gall proved that the brain consisted of separate areas and was not a unified organ, as others had believed. However, Gall went on to develop phrenology, the theory that mental development influenced the shape of the brain and was reflected in the shape of the skull. He believed that the bumps on one's head were clues to one's mental capacities. Phrenology was found to be totally unfounded and was dismissed as quackery. Gall is now usually limited to a footnote in the history of neurological science, an example of a genius gone astray, even though he stayed within his own discipline.

A similar case is that of Urbain Jean Joseph Le Verrier, the astronomer who discovered the planet Neptune in 1846. Upon studying the irregularities in the orbit of the planet Uranus, Le Verrier concluded that they were the result of another planet's gravitational influence. Le Verrier's prediction of where this other planet would be was soon confirmed. This discovery brought him great honor. Several years later, after studying irregularities in Mercury's orbit, Le Verrier predicted the presence of another unknown planet. In this case, however, his prediction was incorrect, no planet was ever found, and his stature received a crippling blow. So, even though a person of genius remains within his or her area of expertise, there is no guarantee that he or she will intuit the significant problems in that area.

Perhaps the most striking example of a scientific genius making the wrong choice on a scientific problem is Einstein's reaction to the uncertainty principle of quantum mechanics. One of Einstein's most profound insights was his postulation in 1905 of the particle nature of light, or the light quantum. For 200 years, most physicists believed light existed in the form of continuous waves, and then Einstein, in a throwback to much earlier ideas, claimed that it was made up of individual particles, or quanta. His elaboration of this idea led to great developments in physics, including a long-lasting controversy between the proponents of the wave versus particle views of the nature of light. One of the most important of these developments was quantum mechanics, the study of the laws governing the behavior of light quanta and other particles.

As work progressed on the laws of quantum mechanics, a basic problem was discovered in determining the precise position and velocity of a particle at a specific instant in time. The work of several of the most important physicists in the first quarter of the twentieth century led to the view that it was *impossible* to measure precisely the behavior of particles, because to do so one would need to "see" them. In order to see the particle, one would have to use light, or particles, which would collide with the particle one wished to measure, thereby changing its position and/or its velocity. Thus, the very act of measuring the position and velocity of a particle changed the quantities one wished to measure, making it impossible to ever measure those quantities precisely. This meant that the laws of quantum mechanics had to be statistical laws, rather than precise deterministic laws. That is, if one knew the position of a car, and the speed and direction of its movement at a particular instant, then one could use these initial calculations to determine where the car would be at any subsequent instant in time. The theorizing in quantum mechanics showed that this determination did not hold at the level of atomic particles. The best one could do was to say that with a certain probability the particle was here, or there, or wherever.

This change, from strictly deterministic to probabilistic or statistical laws, resulted in a basic change in the foundations of physics. Although probabilistic laws are accepted today, they were not accepted by many physicists at the time they were proposed. Einstein was among the physicists who resisted the notion of statistical laws, and throughout his life believed that eventually a way would be found to develop strictly deterministic laws governing the behavior of particles. Einstein encapsulated his strong opposition to the probabilistic view in a famous statement made in a letter to a fellow physicist, Max Born, in December 1926.

> Quantum mechanics is certainly imposing. But an inner voice tells me that it is not yet the real thing. The theory says a lot, but does not really bring us any closer to the secret of the Old One [i.e., to understanding how God created the world]. I, at any rate, am convinced that He does not throw dice.

That is, Einstein could not accept the conclusion quantum mechanics seemed to lead to, that there was no precise way to determine where a particle would be at a given point in time.

The important point about Einstein's rejection of the statistical laws of quantum mechanics is that these laws are now accepted as the basis for the modern physicists' conception of the universe. Einstein's rejection of quantum mechanics can thus be seen as a failure of his "sensitivity to problems," since it became an area that led to fruitful work. As Einstein himself put it, his rejection of quantum mechanics resulted in his being moved from the forefront of theorizing in physics, "a genuine old museum piece." It should also be mentioned again that quantum mechanics came about as an extension of work Einstein himself initiated. Interestingly, this means that Einstein began modern theorizing about particles without being able to see far enough into the future to predict where it would lead.

It should be noted that Einstein's rejection of quantum mechanics was probably not because his personal characteristics had changed in any fundamental way from the time when he did his revolutionary work. On the contrary, his basic belief in determinism and in strict causal laws motivated both his earlier work and his rejection of quantum mechanics. Thus, the same personal characteristics can lead an individual to a creative breakthrough of revolutionary proportions *and* result in that same individual's resistance to the breakthroughs of others. The same personal characteristics can be those of genius, or of an "old museum-piece." Similar examples can be found in the careers of other scientists, but since Einstein is looked upon by many as the most creative and greatest genius of modern science, his case is by far the most interesting.

In summary, if sensitivity to problems is a characteristic of scientific genius, there is abundant evidence that some of the greatest scientists in history failed to exhibit this characteristic uniformly throughout their lives. Thus, the concept of enduring genius is called into question from yet another direction.

These examples can also be used to disprove another intuition concerning genius: even the greatest scientists are not uniformly creative throughout their lives. Einstein's lack of creative thinking was not due to his leaving his domain of expertise or somehow changing the way he saw things. On the contrary, the characteristics that were crucial in producing his earlier revolutionary work also made it difficult for him to adjust to the changes that occurred as theory in physics evolved. This is very important in the present discussion, because it indicates the impossibility of isolating the personal characteristics that are necessary for a person to possess genius. The personal characteristics important in a scientist's producing creative, influential work (i.e., in a scientist's exhibiting "genius") depend on which problem the scientist is trying to solve. The same characteristics that contribute to work of genius in one case may result in an inability to even begin to think in a constructive way about a problem in another.

Leonardo da Vinci, another example of genius, is celebrated for a life full of creative achievements in science and the arts. Leonardo is the classic example of the type of individual Barron refers to when he talks about "a lifetime of original thinking." We are all familiar with Leonardo's work on flying machines and his studies of anatomy, but his notebooks are filled with ideas about many topics, ranging from weapons of war to the design of stables. It is also true, however, than an examination of Leonardo's life and work reveals that he also made his share of mistakes, some of which were major. In his experiments on human flight, for example, he spent years trying to perfect a flying machine that flew by flapping its wings. In addition, he developed a new method of painting on plaster which allowed him to paint his fresco of the *Last Supper* at a more leisurely pace, but unfortunately, this method resulted in the paint fading prematurely, so that the *Last Supper* is in relatively poor condition today.

Examination of Leonardo's notebooks reveals other examples of this sort, which simply proves that even the greatest scientists and inventors among us are still human and, as such, are fallible. Therefore, the belief that genius is a constant characteristic is once again brought into question.

One could summarize the discussion in the last several sections by saying that an individual's exhibition of scientific genius depends on at least two things: the particular individual involved and the particular scientific environment he or she is placed in. To recapitulate, using Einstein as an example, Einstein exhibited genius in an area that was amenable to the sort of strict deterministic analysis with which he was comfortable. When theorizing in physics shifted to laws of a statistical nature, however, he was left behind. It is perhaps not too far-fetched to surmise that if Einstein had been born twenty years later (and assuming that relativity theory and quantum mechanics had developed in the same way without him), he would not have exhibited genius in physics. That is, either he might have tried in vain to provide a set of deterministic laws to substitute for the statistical laws of quantum mechanics, or he might not even have been interested in a career in physics at all because quantum physics would not have resembled the way he felt comfortable thinking about physical phenomena.

If it is true that the crucial personal characteristics determining genius in a scientist depend upon the problem being considered, and if it can be assumed that there are many types of problems in science, then there must be many ways to be creative in science. If so, then many different sorts of characteristics must be relevant to scientific genius. To put it another way, if many different sorts of characteristics comprise scientific genius, then the idea of scientific genius, i.e., a set of core characteristics common to all creative scientists, is a myth.

Is the Artistic Genius Always Creative?

There is a striking parallel between the discussion of the constancy of scientific genius in the last few sections and the question of the constancy of artistic genius. Creative artists of the highest order also fail to exhibit constancy of creativity throughout their careers. In addition, artistic genius can wax and wane even after an artist's productive career is over, which raises other important implications for our understanding of the concept of genius.

All artists experience great fluctuations in the quality of their work. No artist produces only masterpieces. Wayne Dennis's analysis of the careers of well-known composers reveals an essentially constant relationship between the production of major and minor works. That is, in the periods in which composers produce relatively large numbers of major works, or works of genius, they also produce large numbers of minor works. Dennis classified works into major and minor on the basis of their being discussed in music reference works.

This finding has two important implications in the present context. It indicates that constancy of genius throughout a career does not occur, even at the highest levels of musical creativity, and it raises some interesting questions about the alleged sensitivities of genius. If a genius produced a piece of work, presumably he or she would believe that it was worthy of publication and was not simply a way to earn some money. If posterity deems the work a minor work, however, then the artist's judgment is mistaken. This raises the possibility that the artist of genius, contrary to our culture's beliefs, is not particularly sensitive to the responsiveness of the audience. Even the greatest artists may simply be producing for themselves and not for others.

If one responds to a work of art, it seems reasonable to assume that one was affected directly by some element of the work. Furthermore, it also seems reasonable that the artist put that element into the work because he or she knew it would move the audience. Such a work is called creative, and the capacity of the artist to produce such a work is called genius. There are, however, a number of reasons why these beliefs about artistic creativity and genius are false. First and foremost, artistic genius depends on the response of an audience. Upon tracing the judgments accorded to some artists by posterity, one finds interesting cases in which the artist's reputation changed radically over the years. Such cases are crucial in analyzing the nature of artistic genius.

As an example of the sometimes fluctuating nature of the reputation and influence of an artist, let us briefly consider the posthumous reputation of Johann Sebastian Bach. Although Bach is presently regarded as one of the greatest composers who ever lived, his reputation was not always so exalted. When Bach died in 1750, public performance of his works essentially died with him and his music was ignored for about seventy-five years. Even Bach's own composer sons dismissed their father's work as hopelessly old fashioned, and referred to him as "the old wig." It was not until the early 1800s that interest in Bach's music revived, although the performances were seldom in the authentic Baroque style. It was not until relatively recently that musicians returned to playing Bach's works as he himself might have played them.

Here is the paradox: an artist whom we honor as a musician of undeniable genius was ignored for seventy-five years after his death. If one believes that artistic genius includes the capacity to create in one's work elements that produce universal emotional responses in an audience, then how can Bach be classified as possessing musical genius when earlier generations dismissed him as having essentially no value? Bach's works have not changed since his death, and the elements that move us today existed in 1800 when the work was thought to be worthless. It appears that the elements that serve at one time as the basis for acclamations of genius, can at other times support the classification as a hack. Furthermore, whatever personal characteristics Bach possessed that determined how he wrote music, served at one and the same time to produce music of genius (i.e., the characteristics were those of a genius) and music of no value (i.e., the characteristics were those of a hack).

This analysis leads one to conclude that those who believe artistic genius involves a special set of unchanging personal characteristics have overlooked something important: the sensibility of the audience. An artistic work becomes a work of genius only when it moves an audience, and the tastes of the audience can change. Any attempt to locate genius in either the artist or the work alone is doomed to failure, therefore, because genius is the interaction between a work of art and the sensibility of an audience. Genius is not a personal characteristic like eye color. Eye color essentially does not change and can be measured reasonably objectively. The same is not true of genius—genius is a characteristic that is *bestowed upon* an individual through the subjective response of an audience. Possessing genius is much like possessing beauty—it depends on who is doing the judging.

A believer in the absolute nature of genius might argue that Bach did possess special "genius" characteristics which were indeed expressed in his music. For some unknown reason, however, the generations immediately after Bach's death were insensitive to it. Further evidence for the interactive nature of genius can be found in studying the factors that played a role in bringing about the Bach revival. According to an analysis in *The New Grove Dictionary of Music and Musicians,* the rekindling of German interest in Bach's music was only one facet of a more general interest in German tradition. This general interest, in turn, may have been generated by the military and political humiliations Germany suffered during the Napoleonic period. Initial interest in Bach, therefore, occurred because he was German, and not because he was Bach. His great creative output was looked upon as a national treasure. A biography of Bach, written by J. N. Forkel in 1802, early in the Bach revival, makes this nationalistic aspect very clear.

> This great man was German. Be proud of him, but be worthy of him too . . . . His works are an invaluable national patrimony with which no other nation has anything to be compared.

Thus, the revival of interest in Bach can be seen to have resulted from a very complicated set of sociohistorical circumstances. In this light, it is almost meaningless to claim that Bach composed for later generations. One would have to believe that Bach had been in some way able to anticipate the very complicated forces that made audiences sympathetic to his work. It is much more plausible to say that Bach simply composed as he composed and that what he produced struck a responsive chord 100 years later.

Another example of how little is added by saying that an artist works for future generations is seen in the relatively recent revival in the music of Scott Joplin. In this case, the stimulating set of circumstances involved the use of Joplin's music in the motion picture *The Sting,* whose huge success thus exposed many people to Joplin's music. The positive emotional content of the motion picture also may have fostered a positive reaction to the music. The essentially accidental nature of these events is obvious, and it explains very little to say that Joplin composed for later generations. How could he know what later generations would be like? Again, Joplin composed as he composed, and his popularity (and his "genius") waxed and waned.

This analysis leads to one further question. If artists really have no idea of the factors that will affect later generations' response to their work, why do they say things like: "It is not done for you, but for your children's children?" There are several possible reasons for such statements. If an artist produces original work that is outside the mainstream, then he or she knows it will take time, perhaps a long time, before audiences assimilate it. The artist has not said much more than "It just takes some time to get used to," and he or she may be doing nothing more than expressing a hope. What else could one say when a lifetime had been invested in the production of a body of work and it was being denigrated by critics and audiences alike?

We are left with the conclusion that no specific characteristics underlie artistic genius, and that the search for artistic genius is based on the incorrect notion that *being* a genius involves *possessing* genius. We are still left with a very important question, however: Why are some artists acknowledged by posterity as geniuses and others are not?

There are two related points to be made in response to such a question. First, there is no guarantee that posterity's judgments are permanent. It is possible that today's artists of high esteem may be discarded by future generations. There may not be any difference between the genius and the nongenius as regards the characteristics of their work, since the very same characteristics can at one time be valued and at another be considered worthless. Second, to extend this line of reasoning, if genius depends on posterity's response, then the only difference between the genius and the nongenius may be the audience's response to their work. Assume for the sake of discussion that two artists spend their careers in the same area. Both are skilled workers, both are committed to their careers and produce what they believe is high-quality work. One artist is acclaimed, however, while the other is not. To continue our discussion further, perhaps the only difference between the two artists is that one was fortunate enough to produce works that evoked a positive response, while the other was not. That is, perhaps neither artist was exceptionally sensitive to the audience or had any insight as to which works would be judged to possess genius. Each artist simply produced work he or she found satisfying, and the sensibilities of one of them matched those of the audience.

It is helpful to compare judgments of genius to judgments of beauty. Consider photographs of two individuals, one of whom is judged to be beautiful and one whom is not. In both cases, the individual's facial configuration developed as a result of genetic factors. In neither case was anything the individuals did, nor anything in the psychological structure of the individuals, causally related to the ultimate judgments of beauty. The same may be true of artistic production and genius. Getzels and Csikszentmihalyi believe that an individual decides to become an artist because it allows him or her to exhibit a degree of control over the world. Thus, the individual becomes an artist to meet certain inner needs, and presumably the work he or she produces also serves to meet those needs. Because there are probably as many specific sets of needs and ways of meeting these needs as there are people, each artist develops an individual style in which his or her experiences and personality play a role. This parallels the factors involved in the development of an individual's face. The next step is the exposure of the artist's work to the scrutiny of society, and if a given individual happens to work out his or her personal issues in a way that others can respond to, that person will be acknowledged a genius, at least temporarily.

To summarize, there is nothing intrinsically unique about an artist to make them possess genius; *we*, their audience, bestow genius upon them.

Summary

This chapter considered whether there are characteristics of creative individuals that could be called genius, and whether these characteristics could in some way be instilled in others in order to make them creative. Evidence of several sorts called the assumptions underlying the concept of genius into question. First, creative individuals within a given field may not possess a set of characteristics that differentiate them from noncreative individuals with similar backgrounds within the same field. Second, psychological characteristics may not be causally related to later creative work. Third, creativity is not constantly exhibited even by the greatest artists and scientists, indicating that genius is not a constant characteristic. Finally, an analysis of the broader aspects of the concept of genius indicate that it is a mistake to look for genius either in an individual or in an individual's work. Rather, genius is a characteristic that society bestows upon an individual in response to his or her work. Since the sensibilities of society change, so do its judgments of genius. A person who was considered to possess genius at one time might at another time be dismissed by posterity. If this is true, then looking at the characteristics of an individual, in order to determine the basis for genius, must be doomed to failure.

6

THE MYTH OF
SCIENTIFIC CREATIVITY

Great scientific discoveries have profound effects on every aspect of our lives, and the discoveries discussed in this chapter—Darwin's theory of evolution and the discovery of the structure of DNA—are clear examples of this. Darwin's theory of evolution through natural selection raised questions about the validity of religious beliefs important to Victorian society and about the position human beings held in the world, questions which arouse strong emotions even today. The discovery of the structure of the DNA molecule played a central role in a series of revolutionary advances in biology, one of which, the creation of new life forms, has wide-ranging implications for our lives. In these cases, and obviously in many others, the world has been drastically changed because of the creative work of scientists.

Perhaps because of this widespread influence of scientific theories, there is sometimes a tendency to take a very romantic view concerning the processes involved in scientific creation. Descriptions of scientists' creative thinking often emphasize the adventure involved, i.e., the theorist venturing alone into unknown territory, relying on nothing more than scientific intuition. Because the results are so extraordinary, it seems reasonable to assume that the thought processes are extraordinary as well.

The following is a description by James Adams of the work of James Watson and Francis Crick, the discoverers of the structure of DNA.

> Watson and . . . Crick relied heavily on inspiration, iteration, and visualization. Even though they were superb biochemists, they had no precedent from which they could logically derive their structure and therefore relied heavily on left-handed [intuitive, nonlogical] thinking.

Adams emphasizes the fact that Watson and Crick could not rely on past work, and so were forced to use their intuition to create something completely new. According to Adams, Watson and Crick apparently plunged into the unknown on their own without guidance from earlier scientific work.

Other writers also have told of creative scientists working independently of what was already known. Indeed, great importance is sometimes placed on the fact that such men and women lacked formal education, because formal education is assumed to stifle the creative processes. Lack of education presumably leaves the scientists' thought processes more "free," since they do not become wed to the old way of thinking about things. An example of this view is seen in the following quote, from Edward De Bono.

> Many great discoverers like Faraday had no formal education at all, and others, like Darwin or Clerk Maxwell, had insufficient to curb their originality. It is tempting to suppose that a capable mind that is unaware of the old approach has a good chance of evolving a new one.

This chapter subjects this view of scientific creativity to critical analysis by examining two case histories of scientific discovery in detail. I shall try to show that scientists do not make great intuitive leaps into the unknown independently of what has come before, but that even in its most impressive manifestations, scientific discovery develops incrementally and is firmly based on the past. The discussion addresses the following sorts of questions. Why was the scientist interested in the phenomenon in the first place? What ideas concerning the phenomenon were already available? What was the relation between the new discovery and the old ideas? Did the new discovery unfold all at once, or as a series of steps? How did the discovery develop; did it grow from one single line of thought or were there backtrackings and changes of direction and, if there were, what brought these changes about?

I hope to show that scientific thinking progresses in a manner not unlike that involved in solving the Charlie and candle problems discussed in Chapter 1. In both cases, subjects first attempted to solve the problems directly, based on their knowledge of the problem situation or situations like it. Creative solutions developed as the problem solvers acquired information indicating that their initial solutions were inadequate. In attempting to overcome these inadequacies, subjects were led to try things they had not tried before.

For the present discussion, the important points are that the initial attempt to solve a problem depends relatively directly on what the person knows about the problem when he or she starts working. Changes in the way the person approaches the problem (that is, "restructurings") occur in response to information that becomes available as the person works on the problem. That is, restructurings are not intuitive leaps into the unknown, but responses to changes in the problem. Finally, novel solutions to problems also arise in response to information that becomes available as the person works on the problem.

In addition, it is sometimes argued that scientific genius is somehow blessed with an intuitive sense of just which scientific problems are both potentially important *and* solvable. According to this view, the nongenius either spends time solving problems that are not particularly important, or tries to solve those that turn out to be unsolvable or not easily solvable. By considering the backgrounds of creative scientists, I hope to show that their interest in the problem that made them famous evolved naturally from the social and intellectual environment in which they developed. Once again, no extraordinary processes are needed to explain why the scientists were interested in certain problems. The problems in question were "in the air" at the time, and they were not the only scientists to see the potential importance of those problems.

Thus, this chapter attempts to demonstrate that the thought processes involved in two important scientific discoveries were not very different from those used by ordinary people dealing with small problems. Chapter 7 presents a similar discussion of creative thinking in the arts.

Restructuring in the Discovery of the Double Helix

One particularly clear example of restructuring in scientific discovery is seen in Watson and Crick's discovery of the structure of the DNA molecule. The double helix of DNA, shown in Figure 6.1, is found in every introductory text in genetics, psychology, biology, and many related fields. Watson and Crick's discovery helped bring about the recent revolutionary advances in molecular biology and genetics. The discovery of the double helix did not unfold smoothly in a single direction, however, there were a number of false starts and much revision of early ideas before things finally fell into place.

Watson, who was in his early twenties when this work was conducted, had already received a Ph.D. in genetics from the University of Indiana. Watson's professor, Salvador Luria, believed that understanding how the genes controlled heredity depended on understanding their chemical structure. Watson was therefore sent to the laboratory of Herman Kalckar, a Danish chemist. While in Europe, Watson attended a scientific meeting where he saw an X-ray of DNA in crystal form, taken by Maurice Wilkins, an X-ray crystallographer from King's College, London. X-ray crystallography is the "photographing" of crystals using X-rays. The technique involves taking a crystal of some substance and exposing it to a concentrated X-ray beam. The X-rays are deflected by the atoms in the crystal and the pattern of deflection is recorded on film, since X-rays will expose film. The procedure is also called X-ray diffraction because the X-rays are diffracted by the crystal. When the exposed film is developed, an expert can tell from the pattern formed by the X-rays how the atoms in the crystal are organized.

Wilkins's picture excited Watson greatly, because it showed him that genes could crystallize, or form into crystals, like salt crystals. In order for this to occur, the molecules of the material must be able to combine in a uniform way. If so, genes must have a regular structure that can be analyzed reasonably directly. At about this time, Linus Pauling, the internationally famous chemist, had proposed that the molecular structure of a protein was a long chain of atoms, which formed a helix (the shape of a spiral staircase). Pauling's work made Watson even more interested in learning how to work with X-ray diffraction in order to take pictures of crystals, so he obtained a position at the Cavendish Laboratory in Cambridge, England.

The Cavendish Laboratory was directed by Sir Lawrence Bragg, who had won the Nobel Prize thirty-five years earlier for his work in X-ray diffraction. Bragg and his colleagues had been applying this method in order to analyze larger and

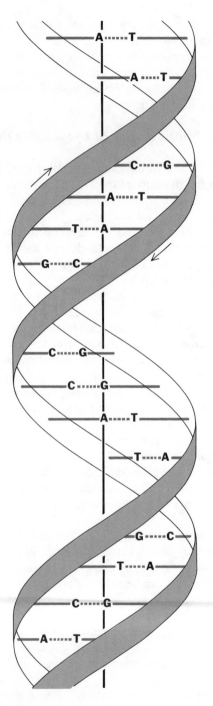

Fig. 6.1
The double helix.

larger molecules. Crick had been on the staff at the Cavendish Laboratory for several years when Watson arrived, and was familiar with the use of X-ray diffraction, and considered it an important tool. A Ph.D. student in his mid-thirties, Crick had been trained in physics (as had Bragg) and was especially interested in developing theories concerning the structures of complex molecules. Thus, Pauling's work had impressed both Crick and Watson, and both had much interest in "solving the problem" of the structure of DNA. Crick had also seen Wilkins's X-ray of DNA, and had talked to him about the molecule's possible structure.

Thus, when Watson and Crick met at Cambridge University in the fall of 1951, both of them believed that solving the problem of the structure of DNA was a task of great importance. This belief had been fostered by the scientific milieu in which each of them developed.

They then faced the question of where to begin. They took their general method from Pauling's work, which involved building models of molecules, and this pointed to the important evidence provided by X-ray photography concerning the structure of molecules. In addition to the general method of building molecular models, Pauling also provided some specific information about the kinds of structures that might be important. Since Pauling's helical model had already been successful, and because other possible structures would be much more complicated than a helix, Watson and Crick decided to try to model DNA using helical models. They set out to build a model of the DNA molecule that was consistent with all that was known about DNA at the time. This included information from studies of its chemical composition, the sunburst patterns of X-ray photographs which revealed bits and pieces about the shape of the molecule, and evidence from genetic studies on how DNA worked during reproduction.

Given their backgrounds and knowledge, it is not hard to understand why Watson and Crick chose to work on DNA in the way they did. These facts raise questions about the Adams claim that Watson and Crick had "no precedent" to work from. Pauling and Bragg provided much in the way of methods and Pauling provided specific starting points concerning possible structures. As will be shown, still other information was provided by other scientists.

These preliminary decisions led to several further questions for Watson and Crick. First, how many strands should the helix contain? There was evidence from X-ray photographs that the molecule was thicker than a single strand, but did it contain two, three, or four strands (Figure 6.2)? There also was the question of whether the backbones of the strands were located on the inside or outside of the molecule (Figure 6.2). In a spiral staircase, the backbone is located on the outside and the steps of the staircase are located on the inside. The steps of the staircase can be considered equivalent to the *bases* of the DNA molecule, which actually carry the genetic message. It was also possible, however, that the backbones were located inside the molecule and the bases on the outside.

Near the end of November, 1951, Watson and Crick built their first model, a three-stranded helix with bases on the outside. This model was based on various pieces of information that were available about DNA, perhaps most importantly

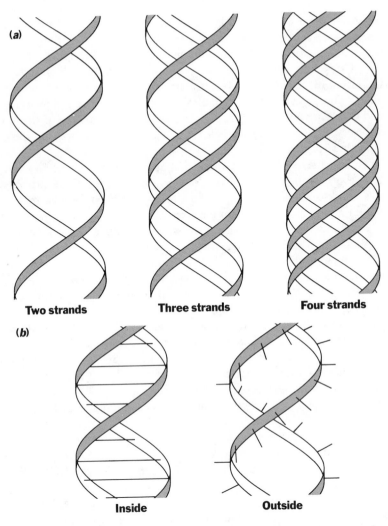

(a)

Two strands   **Three strands**   **Four strands**

(b)

Inside   **Outside**

Fig. 6.2
(a) Multiple-strand helices. *(b)* Possible positions of bases.

on work being conducted by Wilkins's group at King's College. These two teams were more-or-less friendly rivals. Watson recently had attended a lecture by Rosalind Franklin, one of Wilkins's colleagues, in which she discussed X-ray pictures of DNA and the amount of water present in the molecule. Watson and Crick discussed Franklin's results (or, rather, they had discussed Watson's memory of them) and decided to start with a three-strand, center-backboned model because they felt that only such a structure would be regular enough to produce the clear X-ray pictures that the King's group had obtained. The specific shape of the helix, with the three backbones twisting about each other, was designed to enable it, among other things, to hold the amount of water Franklin reported.

Soon after this initial model was completed, the King's group visited Cambridge to see it. The meeting was a disaster for Watson and Crick. First and foremost, Watson misrecalled Franklin's report of the amount of water in DNA, so the model contained only one-tenth of the necessary water. This and other problems made it obvious that this three-stranded model was simply incorrect.

To summarize this initial phase of Watson and Crick's work, they adapted Pauling's method and attempted to apply it to a similar type of problem. The initial solution was inadequate and they were forced to modify it.

Over the next fifteen months or so, basic changes took place in Watson and Crick's thinking and model building. The three-strand, center-backbone model became a two-strand, outside-backbone model. Thus, two restructurings took place—in the number of strands, and the location of the backbones. How did they come about?

As far as the position of the backbones was concerned, several further pieces of evidence pointed to an outside-backbone structure. First, late in 1951, as Watson and Crick tried to revamp their three-strand inside-backbone model to deal with the problems raised by the King's group, all the inside-backbone models they devised violated basic laws of chemistry. In order to build an inside-backbone model, atoms had to be put closer together than the laws of chemistry allowed. This problem probably impressed Watson and Crick greatly, because much of Pauling's work had been spent accurately measuring the distances between atoms in molecules. With their knowledge of Pauling's work, therefore, Watson and Crick would very likely have worried about distances between atoms. Second, early in 1952, Wilkins wrote to Crick saying that he was almost certain the backbones were on the outside. Third, in January, 1953, Watson saw a new X-ray photograph of DNA made by Franklin and, to the expert eye, the backbones were clearly on the outside. (Watson learned to read X-ray photographs in 1952.)

During this time, other factors began to point more and more strongly to a two-stranded structure rather than three strands. First, several other investigators working on three-strand models had also failed to produce anything. Indeed, early in 1953 Pauling himself proposed a three-strand, center-backbone model, much like Watson and Crick's, and it turned out to be just as wrong. Second, though the two-strand structures would not contain as much water as Franklin's measurements indicated, it was possible that her measurements were incorrect, which would make two-strand structures more plausible. Third, information in a report by Franklin indicated that the backbone chains came in pairs and ran opposite to each other, leading one to expect two chains rather than three. Of course, it was possible that there were four, six, or eight strands, etc., but if there were an even number of strands, two seemed the obvious place to begin model building. Finally, one reason why Watson had not wanted to try outside-backbone models was because he had not been able to see how to fit the bases inside so that the structure would be regular enough. As a rough analogy, Watson was trying to build a spiral staircase, but he was not sure that all his steps were the same size. With different-sized steps, the helix would be irregular, would wobble, and would not produce clear X-ray pictures. Early in 1953, however, the models of the bases were not yet available from the machine shop in the Cavendish Lab, and Watson could ignore the bases and try to construct a two-strand, outside-backbone helix that would fit the evidence available.

To summarize the work so far, the initial model was abandoned because of various problems with it. These problems, as well as several new pieces of data, led Watson and Crick to begin work on a different type of model. The two crucial restructurings took place in response to changes in the problem situation.

Watson had little trouble constructing a two-stranded helix without bases, which, if DNA were similarly constructed, would account for Franklin's X-ray photographs. The next question involved the bases—a way had to be found to fit them together to form the steps that held the backbones together. Once again a restructuring had to take place, and once again the restructuring occurred in a straightforward way.

Watson first tried putting the bases into the center of the model one way, but this turned out to be incorrect. He had tried to pair bases of the same type, called "like-like" pairing, to make the steps which would hold the backbones together. The problem was that the various bases were of different sizes, so that when put together, the steps were also of different sizes, and the backbones could not be the same distance apart at all points. There were additional reasons for rejecting the like-like method, so Watson then tried various combinations of different pairs of bases, essentially by trial and error, until he found the needed combinations. Here is how Watson describes the final steps.

> When I got to our still empty office the following morning, I quickly cleared away the papers from my desk top so that I would have a large, flat surface on which to form pairs of bases held together by hydrogen bonds. Though I initially went back to my like-like prejudices, I saw all too well that they led nowhere. When Jerry came in I looked up, saw that it was not Francis, and began shifting the bases in and out of various other pairing possibilities. Suddenly I became aware that an adenine-thymine pair held together by two hydrogen bonds was identical in shape to a guanine-cytosine pair held together by at least two hydrogen bonds. All the hydrogen bonds seemed to form naturally; no fudging was required to make the two types of base pairs identical in shape . . . . Upon his arrival Francis did not get more than halfway through the door before I let loose that the answer to everything was in our hands.

While fiddling with the base models, Watson saw that two specific pairings produced steps of identical size and would thereby serve to hold the two backbones a constant distance apart. Furthermore, these particular pairings turned out to match the results of earlier studies of the chemical composition of DNA, which was further reason to believe that the pairings were correct. Also, the structure made it easy to understand how DNA replicated itself during cell division, which was still another point in its favor.

In summary, after more than a year of work and thought, the final step in the discovery came about very quietly. The earlier ideas on pairings proved inadequate, which led to another, relatively limited set of possibilities. Watson tried these possibilities until he hit the one that worked.

One obvious aspect of this discovery is how it differs from the romantic view of scientific creativity considered earlier. There were no soaring leaps of insight, no sudden awakenings in the middle of the night with the long-sought solution, no mysterious appearances of ideas from out of the mists of the unconscious. If Watson's account is reasonably accurate (and Horace Judson supports Watson in the points discussed in the last few sections), the sequence of events is very ordinary, much like what happens when an average person tries to solve a simple problem. Based on the backgrounds of the participants, various possible solutions were considered, and modified, until the final solution was produced. As in the various laboratory situations discussed earlier, one can see how the solution evolved in a series of conscious steps, as Watson and Crick worked on the problem. One can also see how the problem changed as they worked on it, as they acquired more information about DNA and learned of the inadequacies of their earlier ideas. In addition, as they got closer to the solution, there were no new methods in their work, nor any striking changes in their results. They went forward a little bit at a time, and sometimes they went backward.

Although this is one of the great discoveries in modern science, the methods are surprisingly ordinary. The *result* is what makes the whole episode extraordinary, not the methods. As one looks at the final product, the DNA model, however, it is sometimes difficult to understand how such a conception could ever be produced by ordinary thought processes. With Watson's report as a guide, however, things become much clearer. Interestingly, Watson reports that when he was struggling with the base pairings, he went to the movies in the afternoons, hoping that the answer would suddenly appear in an illumination as a result of incubation. Nothing came, however, nor did he enjoy the films much because he had trouble forgetting about his work.

It should be emphasized that though one claims no extraordinary thought processes were involved in the discovery of DNA, not just anyone could have produced that discovery. The particular scientists and circumstances involved were unique, and all contributed to the discovery. First, both Watson and Crick were committed to Pauling's model-building method which, although things did not always unfold smoothly, turned out to be very useful. There is some evidence that Rosalind Franklin was also very close to discovering the correct structure of DNA, but one reason that she did not get there when Watson and Crick did may have been that she was less committed to model building. Second, both men felt that solving the DNA puzzle would be of great scientific importance and probably make them scientific immortals—this made the whole undertaking exciting and kept them working at it. Third, coming from different scientific backgrounds enabled them to criticize each other's ideas from a different perspective. Other people at the laboratory in Cambridge also added their expertise at critical times. Finally, both Watson and Crick seemed willing to take risks in their thinking, and while this sometimes got them into trouble, it also ultimately led them in the correct direction.

Thus, when one analyzes the factors that contributed to the discovery of the structure of DNA, one sees that the specific people involved were just one of several factors of critical importance. *These* scientists, working on *this* problem, in *this* setting, produced the discovery. If any of these factors had been significantly changed, someone other than Watson and Crick probably would have made the discovery. This leads to the conclusion that scientific creativity is much more complicated than an isolated genius working on a problem, which supports the analysis of scientific genius presented in Chapter 5. Such complexity is seen even more clearly in the case of Charles Darwin's discovery of the theory of evolution through natural selection. Although Darwin worked essentially in isolation for the fifteen months during which he thought intensively about evolutionary theory, his work also was strongly influenced by that of others.

Darwin and Natural Selection

The theory of evolution through natural selection is sometimes presented as an example of a great scientific discovery occurring in a leap of insight. Indeed, Charles Darwin's *Autobiography* seems to support this view, especially in the following well-known passage in which he discusses how Thomas Malthus's *Essay on Population* influenced his thought. In this essay, Malthus presents the view that any population grows faster than its food supply, resulting in many members of the population being unable to find food. Darwin contemplated Malthus's argument and realized that it meant that some animals which were "more fit" would survive in this competition for food. This in turn would result in these animals passing on their characteristics to their offspring, and so the population would evolve.

> In October 1838, that is, fifteen months after I had begun my systematic enquiry, I happened to read for amusement Malthus on *Population,* and being well prepared to appreciate the struggle for existence which everywhere goes on from long and continued observation of the habits of animals and plants, it at once struck me that under these circumstances favorable variations would tend to be preserved and unfavorable ones to be destroyed. The result of this would be the formation of a new species. Here, then I had at last got a theory by which to work.

Darwin's reading of Malthus allowed him to formulate in essentially complete form the theory of evolution through natural selection. Soon after reading Malthus, Darwin wrote the following in his notebook.

> Three principles will account for all 1. grandchildren like grandfathers, 2. tendency to small change especially with physical change, and 3. great fertility in proportion to support of parents.

This is the encapsulation of the theory of evolution by natural selection. First, each generation passes its characteristics to the following generations. Second, organisms within a given generation vary in many different small ways. Third, because of parental fertility there are many more offspring than parents. This means that offspring must compete for limited resources, and that any variation that helps a given organism compete and survive will be passed on to the next generation. Thus, species constantly evolve due to the "selection" produced by competition.

The passage in Darwin's autobiography, in conjunction with the evidence from the notebook, seems to describe a creative leap to a new theoretical formulation. However, other evidence indicates that the incident was not the leap it appears to be. My description of how the theory of natural selection evolved in Darwin's thinking, hopefully, will show how his views changed over the years as he thought about evolution. Once again, the discussion is concerned with such questions as how Darwin's interest in the question of evolution developed, what ideas were already available, how Darwin's ideas were related to older ideas, and what steps were involved in his formulation of his theory. As occurred with the discovery of the double helix, Darwin did not make steady progress toward his final theory—his early views had to be partly abandoned and partly modified before progress could be made. In addition, Darwin was influenced greatly by the thinking of others, regarding both his general interest in biology and the question of evolution and his more specific views concerning how evolution came about. Before presenting Darwin's discovery, it is first necessary to place it in a historic and social context.

Interest in the possible evolution of species did not originate with Darwin. For several centuries, scientists and philosophers in Europe had been contemplating questions of how species originated and changed over time. As one example of evolutionary theorizing, the work of the Comte de Buffon (1707–1788) is particularly interesting because it probably mentions every significant ingredient in Darwin's theory. Buffon's *Histoire Naturelle*, 1749, discusses the following important factors. First, life sometimes multiplies faster than the food supply, thus producing a struggle for existence. Second, there are variations in form within a single species (no two organisms are identical). Furthermore, these variations are often inheritable and can be taken advantage of by carefully breeding stock. (*Artificial* selection, the human control of animal and plant development through selective breeding, was well-known in Europe long before Darwin.) Third, there is an underlying similarity of structure among animals that are very different, which hints at evolution from a common ancestor. Fourth, long stretches of time are necessary to explain how life on earth developed. Fifth, some animal life has become extinct. Finally, Buffon's overall philosophy is oriented toward an experimental approach to the study of questions concerning evolution.

Buffon is only one example, though perhaps the most striking, of interest in the questions that were to concern Darwin. Furthermore, the tentative answers he proposed were similar to those ultimately proposed by Darwin. Thus, European scientific circles had already developed a deep interest in evolution, which means that Darwin's interest in these questions is by no means extraordinary. Furthermore, Darwin had an even stronger personal reason for interest in evolution due to his family.

Darwin was born in 1809 and died in 1882. During his long life he published many articles and books in addition to *The Origin of Species*. Though he died before Charles was born, his grandfather, Erasmus Darwin, developed a theory of evolution based on the inheritance of acquired characteristics. The elder Darwin proposed that during their struggle for survival some animals developed characteristics that enabled them to adapt better to the environment. These characteristics were handed down to the next generation and evolution thereby occurred. (A very similar view was independently proposed by Jean Baptiste Lamarck, and this general viewpoint is called Lamarckian evolution.) Thus, the problem of evolution was familiar and important to young Darwin, since not only had his grandfather written about it, but the members of his family probably discussed it. In this respect the Darwins were similar to a significant number of people with liberal views who were interested in scientific answers to questions involving the origins and evolution of life on earth.

It is important to contrast the evolutionary view with the prevailing view of the time which relied on the Bible to explain the origins of life on earth. According to the strictest version of the biblical view, all life was brought forth when God created the heavens, the earth, and all living things. One aspect of this literal view of the Bible was that each of the various species was a perfect creation and therefore not subject to change, making any discussion of evolution blasphemous as well as unnecessary. When discoveries of fossils and rock strata raised questions about God's creation, Noah's flood was made to account for them. When it was argued that the organization of multiple fossil layers made it unlikely that they could have been laid down during such a flood, the biblical view was modified to include many floods, of which Noah's was simply the latest. Thus, the orthodox view was that there was no evolution, species were static and unchanging, and periodic catastrophies wiped out all life.

In scientific circles there were many who did not accept this orthodoxy, and Darwin met many such thinkers during his studies at the universities of Edinburgh and Cambridge. He entered Edinburgh University in 1825, to study medicine, but became upset by various aspects of his education and left the university in 1827. While at Edinburgh, he met and became close friends with Dr. Robert Grant, a zoologist who believed in Lamarckian evolution. Darwin and Grant spent much time together and talked about Grant's views on evolution.

Darwin attended Cambridge University from 1827 to 1831. Here, too, he met and was influenced by many important scientists. One of these, John Stevens Henslow, professor of botany and geology, spent much time talking with Darwin and also welcomed him to the weekly open house he held that enabled students and professors to get to know each other and share ideas. Professor Adam Sedgwick invited Darwin on a geologic expedition to north Wales in August, 1831. The scientific techniques of observation and data collection Darwin learned on this trip were important for the rest of his scientific life.

In summary, although Darwin says in his autobiography that he did not get much out of his classes at Cambridge, he seems to have gotten a full education and, by the time he left, was no longer a young man ignorant of modern science. He was able to embark on the next great adventure of his life, the voyage of the *Beagle,* as a scientist sophisticated both in methods of data collection and in modern scientific theory, including modern evolutionary views.

On August 29, 1831 Darwin was offered the post of naturalist on HMS *Beagle,* which was scheduled to carry out a five-year journey around the world, paying particular attention to exploring the shores of South America. The post of naturalist involved collecting and cataloging specimens of animal and plant life. The *Beagle* sailed from England on December 27, 1831 and returned October 2, 1836. During the voyage, Darwin acquired information that convinced him that evolution was a fact, and which set the stage for his attempt to solve the problem of how evolution occurred.

There were two sorts of influences on Darwin during the voyage. The first came from his reading of Charles Lyell's *The Principles of Geology,* and the second came from some of his observations, most particularly those of the animals inhabiting the Galapagos Islands. Lyell's book presented a strong case against the view that science should be based on a literal interpretation of the Bible. Darwin was in the perfect position to gather data concerning phenomena discussed by Lyell in support of the idea that species did not stay the same but continuously evolved. Lyell talked about the competition among plants and animals, and how unhealthy organisms would be destroyed by healthier ones in the "struggle for existence," a phrase that seems to have been used first by Lyell.

Interestingly, Lyell used natural selection as a principle of evolution, but only in a negative manner, as when unhealthy animals lose the struggle. It remained for Darwin to realize that natural selection also worked in a positive manner, since any change that gave an animal an advantage in the struggle for existence would be passed along and thereby result in the evolution of the species. One reason Lyell failed to see this may have been that he was unaware of the tremendous variation that could occur within a species. Darwin became aware of this potential for variation during the voyage of the *Beagle* and therefore was in a position to expand upon Lyell's theory.

As his diary and notebooks show, Darwin was leaning toward a belief in evolution when he left on the voyage, and this idea was strengthened by his observations during the voyage. As the *Beagle* traveled south along the coast of South America, for example, Darwin noted that a series of similar animal groups occurred, with the replacement of one group by another of very similar form. Such a series of similar groups suggested that a single species had differentiated into several highly similar forms. In addition, while exploring the pampas of Argentina he discovered fossils of huge animals that were anatomically very similar to the armadillos existing at that time in the region. This supported the notion that the modern species gradually evolved out of the ancient species. These similarities, which were based on space and time, were somewhat surprising if one believed the literal theologic view that all species were created at once. Why had the creator made these various species so similar? If one believed that these species were related to one another, then these similarities made some sense.

When the *Beagle* reached the Galapagos Islands, a group of approximately twenty islands off the west coast of South America, in September, 1835, Darwin found even more remarkable similarities and differences among species of animals. He collected animals from the various islands and found that the local inhabitants could tell which island each specimen had come from. Thus, the species of animals on these islands differed from each other and were not stable. Darwin was particularly impressed by the various species of finches on the islands, especially the variations among their beaks. Some species had small beaks, while others had large thick beaks, differences which pointed to a great variability within groups of animals, even when the physical environment was essentially identical as it was on these islands. Thus, Darwin was faced with the question of how, by what mechanism, all this variation came about.

In summary, the voyage of the *Beagle* pushed Darwin's thoughts toward the theory of natural selection in several ways. He came to believe that evolution did occur, and he saw that species could vary significantly in their characteristics, even within a constant environment. It is important to keep in mind that during the five-year voyage of the *Beagle,* questions concerning evolution of species were central in Darwin's mind. This provided ample opportunity for his ideas to be changed.

Darwin began two important tasks after his return to England in October, 1836—organizing the material collected on the voyage and thinking systematically about evolutionary theory. In July of the following year he began his first of four notebooks on transmutation of species (evolution), and he formulated his first theory of evolution based on the idea of the "monad." Though this theory is relatively far removed from the theory of natural selection, it is possible to see how and why Darwin changed it until over a year later he arrived at his final theory.

The monad theory is based on the idea that simple living particles, or monads, are constantly springing into life. Monads originate in inanimate matter and are produced by natural forces, so that one does not have to assume that there is a separate supernatural creation for each monad. Each monad has a fixed life span during which it differentiates, matures, reproduces, and dies, becoming a whole group of related species. The simple initial particle becomes more complex over time and ultimately forms the complex organisms living today and preserved as fossils. These organisms respond to changes in the environment with adaptive changes. Thus, changes in the environment produce changes in the monad's "offspring," or evolution. These organism-environment encounters are essentially random, so monad development is irregular. Since not everything that could happen does happen, some evolutionary possibilities do not occur. When a monad dies, all the species it has become die at that same moment. The total number of species stays approximately constant, since when a monad and all its related species dies, new species will develop to replace them.

This theory has components that seem very primitive today, but were accepted at the time. The idea of the spontaneous generation of life from nonliving matter, for example, was not disproved until Pasteur's experiments in 1861. Lamarck also argued that spontaneous generation occurred continuously, while Lyell claimed that species were created in succession and endured for a fixed period. Nor was the monad concept new with Darwin. He took these beliefs and used them as the basis for his formulation of how extinction of species might occur.

Furthermore, at that time, there were several different reasons for believing that extinction occurred through the simultaneous deaths of all the products of a single monad. First, fossil evidence indicated that whole groups of species disappeared suddenly. This "evidence" was actually a mistaken conclusion drawn from imperfections of the geologic record, which in reality is very fragmentary. At the time, however, Darwin accepted it as valid. Second, in order for extinction to come about through *environmental* change, which would make the belief in monads unnecessary, a relatively large-scale change in the environment was needed. This view, a version of catastrophism, which maintained the great upheavals occurred periodically and changed the world drastically, had been rejected by Darwin. Also, if environmental change rather than monad death produced extinction, any change in a species could be erased by a change in the environment. This would mean that there would be no overall evolution. Darwin, therefore, looked for a nonenvironmental cause for extinction (monad lifespan).

Thus, Darwin's monad theory was a reasonable attempt to deal with the facts of species change as he knew them, and it is firmly based on other accepted ideas. Over the next fifteen months or so, great changes occurred in Darwin's thinking, that is the monad theory gradually changed into the theory of natural selection.

Before Darwin was pushed to the theory of natural selection by reading Malthus, a number of changes in his views had resulted in his abandoning the monad theory. These changes came about through his logical analysis of the consequences of his beliefs, new sources of evidence, and a change in emphasis concerning what his theory should account for.

One important aspect of the monad theory was its attempt to account for the origin of life through the development of monads. Darwin's interest shifted to the possibility of life as an ongoing system, however, rather than a system involving the constant creation of new forms. One important factor in this change was the discovery of fossils of unicellular organisms, which meant that some organisms remained simple and that the development of organisms from simple to complex, as assumed by the monad theory, did not always occur. One did not have to assume that all simple organisms alive at present had just been created.

In Darwin's early thinking, the notion of variation among the members of a species was a conclusion drawn from the fact that changes in the environment produce changes in organisms, that monads develop into complex organisms, and that accidental encounters of the organism and the environment result in new evolutionary lines. In Darwin's final theory, variation is accepted as a premise ("tendency to small change . . ."), indicating a basic shift in viewpoint.

There seem to be several reasons for Darwin's shift in opinion concerning the role of variation in his theory. First, a theory of evolution that assumes an inherent tendency for organisms to become more complex and adapt to changes in the environment may say nothing more than evolution occurs simply because it occurs. That is, these assumptions may not address all the important questions of how evolution actually comes about. Also, Darwin became increasingly impressed by the extent of variation in nature, much of which did not seem to be in direct response to environmental change. His experiences on the *Beagle,* especially in the Galapagos, showed him that animals in the same environments can differ, indicating that such variations are not in response to environmental changes. Variation is a given, a fact of organic life.

One thing that became increasingly important in Darwin's thinking is the great fertility (fecundity) in nature, the fact that organisms reproduce at a very high rate. This *super*fecundity was emphasized by Malthus in his *Essay on Population,* but was referred to by other sources as well. The German biologist C. G. Ehrenberg, who was becoming well known in British scientific circles at the time, provided evidence that micro-organisms reproduced at nearly-unbelievable rates. As an example, Darwin wrote in his notebook shortly before reading Malthus that a single micro-organism could produce enough offspring in four days to form a stone of considerable size. Furthermore, the Malthusian idea of large numbers of offspring was discussed by many authors with whom Darwin was familiar, such as Erasmus Darwin and Lyell.

It is important to emphasize again that the idea of natural selection did not originate with Darwin. It was generally acknowledged that deviant organisms tended to be less fit and therefore had less chance of survival. The idea of natural selection as "nature's broom" sweeping away weak organisms had been discussed by many important theorists before Darwin. Darwin's great contribution was the realization that natural selection could also work in a positive direction. In addition, Darwin was familiar with the phenomenon of artificial selection, in which humans breed plants and animals for special characteristics. Though an analogy can be made between the human role in artificial selection and the struggle for survival in natural selection, when Darwin began theorizing about evolution this analogy was not clear to him.

Rather than being a great leap of insight, reading Malthus was simply the final step in a long process during which Darwin's views underwent many changes. These changes in thinking were made up of small modifications based on pressure from new data or logical problems which became apparent to him. Furthermore, the Malthusian insight itself did not originate from nothing, that is, Darwin's views had to change before Malthus could have just the right effect on him.

There is also some evidence that Darwin did not originally perceive his response to Malthus to be a great leap of insight or a profound unveiling of something completely hidden. In the passage from Darwin's autobiography presented earlier, Darwin wrote "it at once struck me . . . ," which leads one to believe that everything fell into place at once. That passage, however, was written many years after the event actually occurred. The entries made in his notebooks fail to indicate that anything particularly momentous occurred. The entry that refers to his reading of Malthus *looks* no different from other entries, and other entries in the notebook made about that time continue to refer to other topics, indicating that Malthus's essay had not produced an illumination that had captured all his other interests. Finally, and perhaps most important, more than a month elapsed before Darwin wrote the "Three principles will account for all" passage cited earlier, in which he succinctly summarized his theory. In other words, there still seemed to be a lot of working out to be done after he read Malthus, and one does not get the feeling that everything suddenly fell into place. Rather, Malthus was just another source of information and ideas which Darwin used as the basis for his thinking.

In conclusion, it seems that when Darwin wrote his autobiography, he may have forgotten exactly what occurred years before. This autobiography also contains another inaccuracy about his thinking. In a passage shortly before the one describing his Malthusian insight, Darwin says that when he started writing his notebooks, he worked without a theory and simply collected facts. The notebooks themselves show this statement to be false because Darwin produced the monad theory very soon after beginning the notebooks. It seems that Darwin wrote his autobiography without consulting his own notebooks.

To summarize, the evidence supports the idea that Darwin's thinking proceeded in a similar manner to that of Watson and Crick. His interest in the problem of evolution was not at all extraordinary; he was acquainted with the thinking of many others in this field, and their ideas were incorporated into his initial monad theory of evolution. The inadequacies of this initial theory required much modification before the theory of natural selection was produced. This modification came about as Darwin's views changed, as he thought more about the consequences of the monad theory, and as he acquired new information about the various phenomena involved. The important thing to emphasize is that there seems to be no need to postulate any extraordinary thought processes in order to understand Darwin's accomplishments. Though he was considering issues of extraordinary importance, he did so in very ordinary ways.

Conclusions

In at least two well-known cases, scientific creativity came about through the same sort of thought processes ordinary people use to solve ordinary problems. In both the discovery of the double helix and the development of the theory of evolution a series of similar phenomena occurred. First, the early theorizing, based relatively directly on ideas of others, was shown to be inadequate in several ways. These inadequacies were addressed by modifying various parts of the old theory, and the result was a new theory. These modifications did not occur all at once in a leap of insight, but rather involved a series of small accommodations as each difficulty was handled. There seemed to be no one point at which everything suddenly fell into place, but rather, there was a gradual closing in on the final theory as bits and pieces fit together. On the whole, the process discussed in this chapter is remarkably similar to the process of creative problem solving discussed in Chapter 1.

The conclusions drawn here are also relevant to the discussion in Chapter 4 about the importance of divergent thinking in creativity, where it was concluded that creative problem solving does not involve suddenly shifting to a new way of viewing the problem. In neither case discussed in this chapter did anything like divergent thinking occur. The theorists involved began with ideas that were readily available in the scientific community, and they modified them to make them relevant to the specific problems they were trying to solve. When the initial formulations were shown to be inadequate, the new directions their thoughts took were not due to anything like divergent thinking, but were the result of the analysis of the new difficulties and the use of additional knowledge and logical reasoning abilities. Nothing like brainstorming seems to have occurred in the discovery of the double helix or the theory of evolution.

Additional studies of scientists also indicate that divergent thinking is not important in scientific creativity. In these studies, scientists of different degrees of creativity were given tests of divergent thinking. The consistent finding in these studies is that performance on divergent thinking tests is unrelated to scientific creativity. That is, the more creative scientists do not perform better on tasks involving divergent thinking, and scientists who do best on the divergent thinking tests are not the most creative in their professions. Thus, divergent thinking does not measure the abilities involved in scientific creativity.

The conclusion developed in this chapter—that creative thinking in science progresses through a series of incremental steps, perhaps in irregular directions —contradicts the generally accepted belief about scientists' thinking process, based on their own reports. Many scientists and creative thinkers in other areas have reported that their creative thinking is often brought about through leaps of insight. This leaves us with a problem regarding these subjective reports; the present analysis does not seem to apply to them. It may be simply that creative thinking occurs in more than one way, the small-step, incremental, revisionist method seen in this chapter, and the insightful-leap method. If this is true, however, it seems surprising that neither of two highly creative scientific discoveries involved such leaps. Furthermore, these two discoveries are extensively documented, making it reasonably clear that neither involved leaps of insight. Also, as Chapter 2 demonstrated, subjective reports of leaps of insight are often very inaccurate sources of evidence. Additional examples of this sort are presented in the next chapter. Thus, whenever extensive documentation is available, such as an individual's notebooks, the evidence tends not to support the subjective reports.

It may be that the difficulty lies with the subjective reports of creative persons and, therefore, the analysis in this chapter does apply to the thought processes in all acts of creativity, scientific and otherwise. Subjective reports are usually difficult to verify because there is seldom any way of knowing if the person is correct or not. There is also evidence of subjective reports being deliberately falsified. Finally, experimental evidence shows that subjective reports can be mistaken. Darwin's report in his autobiography concerning his Malthusian "insight" is a perfect example of a scientist's mistake in a subjective report. When a scientist tries to reconstruct from memory thought processes of a complicated nature that involved emotionally arousing work on an important problem, and which may have occurred many years before, there is a good chance that the reconstruction will be incorrect. If one relies on objective evidence, rather than on subjective reports, then there is no need to postulate leaps of insight. I conclude that the creative individuals who report great leaps of thought were simply mistaken. Since most of those individuals were neither in the business of studying their own thought processes (that is, they were not professional psychologists) nor concentrating on their thought processes at the time of creation, such mistakes are not surprising.

Summary

The two cases discussed in this chapter, the discovery of the double helix and the development of the theory of evolution through natural selection, support the incremental view of creativity outlined in Chapter 1. In both cases, the investigators were initially drawn to the problem because of the importance placed on it in the scientific environments in which they developed. Second, the early theorizing in both cases was a relatively direct extension of ideas available at the time. Because these initial theories were incorrect, a long series of revisions was begun as various aspects were brought into agreement with new information. Finally, the revisions and elaborations of the theories occurred in small steps rather than leaps of insight.

7

THE MYTH OF
ARTISTIC CREATIVITY

In the arts—literature and poetry, drama, music, painting, and sculpture—one finds a set of beliefs concerning creativity quite different from the viewpoint presented so far. First, self-reports by artists contain many instances of creative products springing full-blown into consciousness. It is also generally assumed that these creative leaps are due to unconscious thought processes. Thus, extraordinary thought processes are assumed to underlie creative thinking in the arts. Second, in addition to possessing extraordinary thought processes, the truly creative artist—the artistic genius—is also considered an extraordinary person in other ways. The ability of the creative genius to move an audience emotionally is assumed to be due to his or her extraordinary sensitivity and openness to emotion. This sensitivity is costly, however, because geniuses are believed to walk a fine line between being extremely open and sensitive and being mentally disturbed. Plato wrote of the "madness" of poets, for example, and more modern variants of this are based on the frequency of mental disturbances among great artists. The issue of artistic genius has already been considered in Chapter 5.

This chapter compares this view of the thought processes of the creative artist with available information concerning how they actually work. The discussion is based on two sorts of research: psychological investigations, which have studied artistic production in controlled settings, and analyses of notebooks and sketchbooks left behind by artists. On the most general level, this chapter focuses on the question of the sources of the creative artist's ideas, considering both broad and narrow aspects of their work. Thinking broadly, one can consider the development of new artistic style, such as Alexander Calder's production of the first mobiles or the production of the first collages by Pablo Picasso and Georges Braque. From this broad perspective, the question of an idea's source is one of determining the relationship between the artist's new style and his or her previous work. Did the new style occur as the result of a creative leap and was it therefore independent of what the artist had done before, or is the new style better seen as part of a gradual evolution of the earlier work and therefore traceable back to its roots?

On a narrower scale, the question of the source of the artist's ideas can center on the production of a single work, or group of related works, such as Fyodor Dostoyevsky's *Crime and Punishment* or Ludwig van Beethoven's Ninth Symphony. Do the ideas for such a work, for the plot and characters of a novel or the melodies and structure of a symphony, come to the artist in more or less completed form, or do novels, poems, paintings, and symphonies develop gradually over extended periods of time as the artist works on them? A related question concerns the relative importance of past experience, training, and practice in being able to produce lasting works of art. How important are these factors in the development of artistic capacity?

I believe that the thought processes involved in artistic creativity are of the same sort as discussed in Chapter 1, concerning ordinary individuals solving simple problems, and in Chapter 6, concerning creative scientists solving important scientific problems. The development of a whole new style can be seen broadly as a relatively direct evolution, in incremental steps, out of the earlier interests and work of the artist. Seen more narrowly, individual works of art do not spring full-blown into the artist's head, but evolve as he or she attempts to deal with "problems" in the early versions of the work. In addition, the artistic process is often stimulated by some concrete external event, indicating once again that ideas do not spring from nothing. Finally, there is evidence that the capacity to produce works of art of lasting value depends on years of work, in which the developing artist is first formally or informally introduced to the work and ideas of others and only gradually becomes capable of producing something original of lasting value.

The chapter begins with a discussion of two artistic innovations, the mobile and the collage, in order to investigate the factors that bring about development of a new art form. The discussion then turns to the narrower question of the development of single works of art in poetry, literature, painting, and music. This discussion concentrates on two issues: what thought processes are involved in producing the work and what is the source of inspiration for it? The chapter concludes with a discussion of the role of specific learning experiences in the development of creative talent.

Before discussing specific results, one potentially thorny semantic issue must be considered concerning the definition of a creative leap. This phrase has been mentioned several times already and presumably readers have some idea what it refers to. One of the difficulties in developing a theoretical analysis of creativity, however, is that it is sometimes difficult to agree when a creative leap has been made. That is, two individuals observe the production of a work of art—one is impressed by the artist's production of something novel, and thus classifies the behavior the result of a creative leap, and the second is impressed by the new work's similarity to the artist's earlier work and that of others, and thus classifies the behavior the result of an incremental step beyond anything the artist has done before. Obviously, since these hypothetical observers produced opposite classifications of the same behavior, the problem must lie in the criteria used in their classifications. Therefore, I want to make my own scale of classification explicit at the outset.

One can, for the sake of discussion, propose a "scale of creativity" as the first step in classifying artistic works. Consider a hypothetical situation in which a sculptor simply copies the work of another, adds absolutely nothing to it, and produces so faithful a copy that one cannot tell it from the original. Such a case involves no creativity whatever and the issue of a creative leap never arises. This is one end of the scale. At the opposite end is a person without any musical experience whatever, who, for the sake of discussion, has never even heard music but who one day begins to sing gorgeous melodies. Such a person obviously made a leap since his or her own experience provided no preparation for what was produced.

Because these two examples are hypothetical, they can provide clear-cut points for judgments concerning leaps of creativity. Unfortunately, examples in real life are harder to classify. A more difficult example is the artist who imitates aspects of another's work but never actually copies it. If such an artist were a painter, we might think that we were looking at an unfamiliar painting by Andy Warhol, for example. If the artist were a musician who lived 200 years ago, we might feel that we were listening to an unfamiliar work by Mozart. These examples are useful in defining the first real step on the scale: the artist produces something new, but the style is like that of another.

The next step on the scale involves the development of a style of one's own that has recognizable roots. That is, one recognizes the artist's work and does not confuse it with that of another, but can point to the origins of the style in his or her earlier work and in the work of other artists. One might be able to trace a new work back to other works the artist had done, as well as to works of other artists. Alternatively, one might be able to trace the novel aspect of a new work to modifications the artist performed on an early work. If so, then the new work, or the new style of work, evolved out of earlier work incrementally rather than in a leap.

The next level on the scale involves the production of a new work, or new style of work, that has no recognizable connection to anything the artist did before. Although the artist has experience within the domain in question, there is little or no trace of his or her history in the new work. That is, though one were very familiar with the artist's early work, one would not recognize the new work as belonging to the same artist. In this case, one would say that a leap of creativity was involved.

Based on this scale, the crucial determinant in classifying a work as resulting from step-wise increments versus a creative leap is how strong a case one can make for a connection between the work in question, and what the artist or other artists have done before. I will present several cases to support the claim that whatever an artist produces is always closely related to what he or she, and/or another artist, has done in the past. This is not to say that artists do not produce novel works, but it does say that not even the greatest artist can think in a vacuum. Each great artist puts an individual stamp on what he or she produces, and the greater the artist, the more individual the stamp. This individual stamp, however, is put on material that has come from the artist's experience and is basically a modification of that experience. If the modification is extensive enough and perhaps stretches over a long enough period of time, one may be particularly impressed with the novelty of the work when it is compared to others by the artist. If the intervening steps the artist went through in arriving at the final work were available, however, the novelty of the final work would be much less impressive. This does not mean that the work would be any less valuable as a work of art, it would just be less impressive as a novelty.

Given these preliminaries, we can now consider the broad question of how new artistic forms develop, using as examples the development of mobiles by Calder and the development of collage by Braque and Picasso.

Innovation in Art: The Mobile

Mobiles are found hanging everywhere—above the cribs of newborns, in lawyers' offices, in stores, and in living rooms. They are so common that it is hard to realize that not very long ago there were no mobiles. The name "mobile" was given in Paris in 1932 to the works of the American sculptor Alexander Calder (1898–1976) who is credited with inventing them. Calder's mobiles are hanging pieces of sculpture, constructed so that movement becomes part of the work, with changing configurations of objects coming about as the mobile is moved by air currents or by motors. As a mobile moves, its swinging shapes cut out "chunks" of empty space which become part of the work. In order to understand the development of mobiles, it is necessary to trace some important themes in Calder's career that were present early in his life and which, with some important outside stimuli, came together to produce the mobiles we know today.

Calder came from an artistic family; his mother was a painter and his father and grandfather were famous sculptors. His manual skills were evident very early in the jewelry he made out of wire for his sister's dolls and toys and other gadgets he made for himself. His parents approved of these home-made things and were pleased with their son's activities. This use of wire to fabricate objects was a constant avenue of expression throughout Calder's career, and it played an important part in the development of his mobiles. Calder's mechanical abilities led him to pursue engineering as a career, and he attended Stevens Institute of Technology from 1915 to 1919. Thus, Calder's early life was not involved primarily in art, but in the development and education of his mechanical abilities.

Between 1922 and 1926 Calder attended drawing classes in New York. In 1924, at the age of 26, he began working as an illustrator for the *National Police Gazette*, a periodical, and other free-lance art jobs. One assignment for the *Gazette* involved attending the circus for two weeks and drawing various circus scenes for publication. This exposure to the circus had a lasting influence on Calder's career, and was another factor that led to the creation of mobiles. At about this time he created his first wire sculpture, a sundial in the shape of a rooster; this met a need since he had no clock. Though he had made jewelry and toys out of wire, this was his first attempt to represent an animal.

Calder moved to Paris in 1926 to immerse himself more deeply in an art career. He spent the next several years mainly in Paris, with visits to New York. By this time, two important streams in his work were already present, his use of wire to sculpt animals and his interest in the circus.

Soon after arriving in Paris, Calder began what was to become a life-long project: he began making small movable wood and wire people and animals for a model circus of his own. This interest in making his works move was a third factor leading to the development of mobiles. Calder's circus, which began with a few animal and human performers, gradually expanded until it incorporated tents, multiple rings, tightrope walkers, bareback riders, an exotic dancer, a sword swallower, acrobats, a strong man, animal trainers, stands for spectators, and music. Over the years, Calder gave "performances" of this circus for friends and acquaintances in the art world in Europe and America. These performances brought Calder his first artistic fame. With them several facets of Calder's abilities were combined: his manual talent in sculpting with wire and other media, his artistic ability in creating animals and people, and his engineering ability to design circus performers that could move and perform "tricks."

Between 1927 and 1929, Calder exhibited animated toys, wire animals, and wire portraits of people in galleries in Paris and New York. He also began designing "action toys" that involved movement for an American company. In December, 1929, he exhibited in a New York gallery that also was showing a collection of 18th century mechanical birds in cages. These birds inspired Calder to make his first moving sculpture; wire goldfish bowls in which fish were made to swim about by means of a hand crank operated by the viewer. These goldfish bowls were the first of many variations on movable sculpture he produced, and they were the result of a straightforward coming together of his interest in movement, his construction of circus animals, and his seeing the mechanical birds.

The final steps in the evolution of mobiles as they are known today involved the use of abstract shapes and random wind-generated movement, rather than the mechanical movement of familiar objects. In the fall of 1931, Calder visited the Paris studio of Piet Mondrian, whom he had met when Mondrian attended a circus performance. Mondrian's work was abstract and strongly geometric in its organization, involving white canvases that were divided by black lines into rectangular blocks, some of which were painted in different strong colors. Mondrian's work stimulated Calder in two ways. He began to experiment with abstract painting and drawing, though after two weeks he returned to the materials he felt most comfortable with, those which he could manipulate. Calder did not return to his old style of sculpture, however. The influence of Mondrian was apparent in his new abstract, strongly colored sculptures. When Calder saw Mondrian's blocks of color, he felt that they ought to be in motion, and over the next several years he produced many abstract moving sculptures. These initially were put into motion by hand cranks or motors, but because the motion was relatively restricted without complicated mechanisms, it quickly became repetitive. Therefore, Calder turned to a more natural and unpredictable source of movement—the wind. This resulted in mobiles as we are familiar with them today.

Conclusions   In this brief tracing of Calder's development of the mobile, the gradual evolution of the new form can be clearly seen. Calder's enduring interest in movement and wire materials, combined with important external events such as the circus assignment for the *Police Gazette,* the exhibition of mechanical birds, and Mondrian's abstract painting resulted in the development of moving abstract sculpture. The artistic thought processes involved here, as they are indirectly observed through the work of the artist, do not seem to be in any way extraordinary. No great leaps of artistic intuition are involved. Rather, Calder seems to have approached everything in art from the point of view of an engineer: could it be made from materials that could be shaped by the hand; how could it be made to move? This point of view initially was directly applied to the imitation of moving objects, as in his circus animals and performers and the goldfish bowls. He later applied the technique to abstract objects, which resulted in a new form of sculpture. The thought processes involved here, as evidenced by this evolution, are similar to those already discussed in more detail in Chapters 1 and 6 concerning the production of creative solutions to problems by ordinary individuals and creative scientists. Indeed, it might not be too far-fetched to say that Calder's career involved a long-term exercise in problem solving: How could he apply his particular skills and interests to as wide a range of phenomena as possible?

The Development of Collage

Collage is another type of art which is ubiquitous in our society, almost as ubiquitous as the mobile. Most houses with young children, for example, have a collage attached to the refrigerator door. As with mobiles, we do not usually pay much attention to collage as art, but this now-commonplace medium had its beginnings in the early 1900s, at the hands of important artists.

In the years 1910–1912, Pablo Picasso and Georges Braque began painting in a style called cubism, and collage evolved out of this new style. The cubist style was an attempt to convey multiple perceptions of a single object simultaneously on a single canvas. That is, rather than portray an object as it would be presented in traditional art, from one view fixed in space, the cubists attempted to portray many views of the object at once, including sometimes those from inside the object. This required the artist's breaking the object down into small parts, almost geometric forms, and presenting these various parts from multiple perspectives. Objects portrayed in this way became almost unrecognizable to the untrained eye, as can be seen in Figure 7.1.

Several devices were used to maintain a relationship between the viewer and the object being portrayed. Titles were used to clarify what the object being portrayed was. Simple, everyday objects were often used again and again in cubist still lifes, which enabled the audience to become familiar with the cubist methods of representing reality. A realistic element occasionally was kept in the picture as a sort of humorous signpost. An example of this can be seen in Figure 7.1. Finally, letters or words were occasionally inserted in pictures to help the audience understand the structure of the picture, though these later became part of the picture for their own sake.

Braque soon experimented with more realistic insertions into basically cubist pictures. Perhaps because of his past experience as an interior decorator, he painted very realistic, and very surprising, versions of marble and wood into his paintings. The direct stimulus for this may have been his seeing, in a shop window, wallpaper which looked very much like wood. Thus, the cubists became

Fig. 7.1
Pablo Picasso, *Man with violin*. (Philadelphia Museum of Art: Louise and
Walter Arensberg Collection.)

concerned both with the contrast between the taking apart of visual reality
through cubism and the totally realistic representation of that reality in the same
painting. From here, it was a small step to the introduction of actual fragments
of reality into the paintings, so that instead of painting letters on the canvas, a
newspaper headline would be stuck to it. This led to a deeper interest in the incorporation of common "non-art" materials in paintings, which resulted in
broader attempts to incorporate commonplace objects into works, often in humorous ways.

This sequence of developments parallels that of mobiles. The collage technique did not spring suddenly into the heads of Braque and Picasso, it was their interest in developing a method of representing objects that led them to first incorporate very realistic interpretations of objects and then the objects themselves into their paintings. Once again, the new development was not a great leap into the unknown, but rather an incremental evolution beyond what was done before.

Conclusions   Both of these artistic innovations seem to fall on the "step-wise increment" end of the scale discussed in the introduction of this chapter. In both cases, the innovation depended on long-standing interests of the artists and had been hinted at in their earlier work. There is no need to postulate exotic sorts of thought processes in either case. Though two examples are not enough to base a strong conclusion on, they *do* demonstrate that leaps of creativity do not occur all the time. The availability of detailed information in these cases allows one to move away from the notion of creative leaps to a description of what actually occurred, or at least to a plausible description of what might have occurred. Whether every artistic innovation about which there is detailed information will also turn out to have occurred through incremental evolution remains to be answered.

Let us now turn to the narrower question of whether single works of art come about in a leap of creativity, or whether they also evolve. I hope to show that a given work of art develops over an extended period of time as the artist attempts to solve the problems that arise as work progresses. In addition, I hope to show that the inspiration for a new work of art can be traced directly to incidents in the artist's experience.

Production of a Poem

Experimental studies with poets, as well as the examination of early drafts of poems written by well-known poets, show that poems do not spring full-blown from the brow of the poet. Neither the general structure of a poem nor the specifics such as lines, words, and phrases are all known before the poet begins work. Rather, the process involves extensive reworking and modification of early versions until an acceptable version is finally produced. Poems are subjected to intense critical scrutiny as they are worked on, and even the greatest of them are extensively modified and revised.

One small bit of evidence to support this view came from the discussion in Chapter 2 of Coleridge's *Kubla Khan*. Coleridge claimed the poem came to him all at once during an opium-induced dream. This often-cited example is assumed to be evidence for the role of unconscious processes in creativity. There is evidence, however, that the poem was not conceived as Coleridge reported. There are at least two versions of *Kubla Khan,* and the published version seems to be the later one. If so, then Coleridge reworked the poem before he published it.

Additional evidence of a similar sort comes from the study of original drafts of other poems. A 1984 exhibit at the New York Public Library presented early handwritten drafts of a number of famous poems and all had been extensively revised. The poems, which included work from the last 300 years, ranged from John Donne to Emily Dickinson to T.S. Eliot. An example of such critical revision can be found in the opening lines of the poem "Come, Said My Soul" by Walt Whitman. In one of three drafts the opening line reads "Go, said his soul to a poet, write me such songs." Whitman then substituted "such verse write" for the last phrase, scratched it out and put "go write such songs" in its place, only to scratch it out also. Then he wrote "such songs, such verses write," but this was still not the final version. This sort of revision occurred throughout the poem as Whitman worked through it numerous times until the final version was produced. A *New York Times* article describing this exhibition contained a picture of the first page of one of Whitman's early drafts of this poem. The page is full of crossed-out lines, phrases, and words and is graphic evidence of the extensive amount of work involved in producing even five or ten lines of poetry. As the author of the *Times* article comments, "These poems, encased like rare jewels under glass, make a subliminal statement: that even for the greats, revision was recognized as a necessary element of the creative process."

Controlled studies of poets also support this view. David Perkins had poets write poems in an "artificial" setting, i.e., a laboratory, in which they were asked to bring only an idea for a poem and to think aloud as they wrote so that as much of their work as possible could be scrutinized. In one case, a poet began with the idea that her day was like an air-raid drill, because that was how her children sounded when they cried. She wrote several lines about air-raid drills she remembered from her childhood, but then she had to stop because the connection between her children and air-raid drills was not very strong; in fact, it was connected only by the sound of their wailing. Thus, the beginning of an idea was there, but the core of it was not available. She then worked out in a series of steps the notion that her babies, like the air-raid sirens, were warning her to preserve herself. This was to her a much more satisfactory basis for developing the poem than simply the children's noise. The poet reported the following to Perkins immediately after she realized that the wailing babies and the sirens both told her to preserve herself.

> Well, I was thinking, [reads] *and I am still fighting that cold war/ alone. The wailing babies*—what did they signal me to do? What is it [air-raid siren] a signal for me to do? And actually, (pause) why do you hide? It's because you're trying to preserve yourself, and that's what the babies are signaling me to do too, because basically I can't, I don't tolerate them very well, and it does me in so much that I have to leave them and go into silence, someplace that's silent so I can preserve myself.

This example is important because it indicates that poets, like painters and other artists, do not necessarily know the structure of a work before they start to write. This poet also worked out the deeper meaning in her poem in a series of concrete steps very much like those used in problem solving. Her activity could indeed be called problem solving: she was trying to work out the problem of the connection of air-raid sirens and the wailing of her babies.

To summarize, this analysis of the development of artistic works in poetry supports the view that such works only gradually take their final shape. The artist continues thinking about and revising various aspects of the work until he or she is satisfied. During this process the work may change considerably from the original conception. Further evidence to support this view comes from studies of literature, painting, and musical composition.

Development of a Novel

In a letter to a friend, Fyodor Dostoyevsky described his creative process as follows.

> . . . If you wish—he [the author or poet] is not the creator; life is—the powerful essence of life, the living and essential God, putting his strength in many distinct creations at various places, and most of all in the great heart and in the strong poet, so that if the poet himself is not a creator—(and one must agree with this . . . because certainly a creative work comes suddenly, as a complete whole, finished and ready, out of the soul of a poet) . . .

This passage is a precise formulation of the messenger-of-God view of creativity. Dostoyevsky claims that creative work is done not by conscious action, but in the soul. If one takes his statement as a hypothesis concerning certain extraordinary thought processes in creative thinking, it becomes important to examine evidence from his notebooks to see how he actually worked. Upon examining his novel *The Idiot*, one sees that his notebooks do not support the claims made in his letter.

The Idiot describes the influences of one man on the members of several noble families in nineteenth century Russia. The character is called an idiot by his mother, who despises him. The novel is divided into several parts, the first two of which were especially difficult for Dostoyevsky to write. He seems to have begun with a number of economic and emotional relationships among characters that he then tried to weave into a novel. Dostoyevsky worked on a total of *eight* plans for the first part of the novel as his scheme for the book changed. Furthermore, each of these plans is full of hedges and possible paths, indicating that at no point was he very confident about where the correct direction of the novel lay. Examination of Dostoyevsky's notebooks makes these vacillations clear. After calling one passage in the first plan "the main point," he ends with "or else." Several other passages of this sort are found within the first plan. A passage in the fourth plan is called "the chief idea of the novel," but the next entry is "Well, now there opens up a new path. What is to come now?" Thus, Dostoyevsky's notebooks from the first part of *The Idiot* belie his statement that "a creative work comes suddenly, as a complete whole, finished and ready." Not only were there eight plans for the first part of the novel, none were complete and whole. Indeed, each plan was very tentatively written out, and at the various crucial points in each, Dostoyevsky seemed to have little in the way of an intuitive feeling as to how to proceed.

The second part of *The Idiot* involved Dostoyevsky's attempt to portray what he called a wholly beautiful individual. In a letter to a friend, he mentioned that such an idea had tormented him for a long time, but he was not sure that he could make a novel out of it. Dostoyevsky hoped that the idea would develop "under my pen." Dostoyevsky was aware that other authors had attempted to portray such individuals, such as Don Quixote and Pickwick, but felt that these attempts were only partly successful. Both characters were comic characters and, according to Dostoyevsky, the emotion one feels toward them was not due to their beauty, but because they were unaware of their own goodness. Thus, Dostoyevsky was aware of precedents concerning such a character and he used them, especially the flaw he saw in them, as part of the basis for his own attempt. In Dostoyevsky's view, Christ was the only truly beautiful individual, and he set out to present such an individual in the second part of *The Idiot*. As the following passages from Dostoyevsky's notes show, the characteristics of Christ were used directly as a model for the prince. March 9, 1868: "The Prince forgives everything." March 10: "His way of looking at the world: he forgives everything, sees reasons for everything, does not recognize that any sin is unforgivable, and excuses everything (p. 168)." Finally, on April 10, the entry is: "Prince Christ."

Thus, Dostoyevsky seems to have developed the plan for the second part of the novel by returning to an idea that had interested him for some time. His analysis of the work of other novelists served as the basis for his thinking about his own work and led him to develop a character with Christ-like features. Their work helped him "solve the problem" of how to make his character charming but not comical. In this case, at least, Dostoyevsky's literary imagination, as revealed in his notebooks, worked in very ordinary ways and seems to contradict his own claims concerning the creative process.

Sources in Literature

Though one may accept the view that works of art go through extensive revision before reaching final form, the question of the source of the artist's initial conception remains. One important source is obviously life itself. A novelist's interest in certain general themes can arise from experiences in his or her life, or specific events from a novelist's life can be used more or less directly as part of a novel. As demonstrated in the discussion of the poem about air-raid sirens, specific life experiences can be an important inspiration for poetry.

An example of the role that life experiences can play in the development of a novelist's interest in general themes is seen in Dostoyevsky's *Crime and Punishment*. The novel revolves around Raskolnikov, a poverty-stricken former university student, who robs and kills a mean, dishonest, old woman pawnbroker. During the crime, Raskolnikov is discovered by the pawnbroker's sister, and he then murders her also. The remainder of the novel involves Raskolnikov's reaction to the crime. Raskolnikov initially rationalizes his action because the old woman will not live long anyway, she is doing evil to others, and others will benefit from the money. However, guilt soon begins to torment Raskolnikov, as well as fear arising from the suspicions of a police inspector. The inspector's suspicions grow stronger, although he has no concrete evidence, and Raskolnikov finally is driven to such desperate straits by his guilt and fear that he confesses. The confession brings great relief to him, and he plans to start a new life after serving a prison term.

The main theme of the novel involves the criminal's desire to confess his crime. Although *Crime and Punishment* was written in 1865–1866, this theme also appeared in several of Dostoyevsky's earlier works, mainly in notes for two stories published in 1848. In addition, Dostoyevsky himself was arrested for reading in public a letter considered treasonous by the police. Originally sentenced to death, he was reprieved at the last moment and sentenced to four years of hard labor in Siberia. While suffering in prison, Dostoyevsky spent much time considering a novel based on a criminal's need to confess. Thus, the main theme of the novel may have been motivated in part by Dostoyevsky's personal experiences.

A closely related theme in *Crime and Punishment* concerns Raskolnikov's initial justification of the crime on the grounds that certain extraordinary people are above the laws of society. Raskolnikov considers himself to be like Napoleon, one who shapes the law to his own will, rather than being forced to obey it. This theme also exists in other Russian stories, most notably in *The Queen of Spades* by Alexander Pushkin and *Fathers and Sons* by Ivan Turgenev, both of which Dostoyevsky knew and admired. The Balzac novel *Pere Goriot* also addresses the theme of whether one could kill a useless person and it, too, was well known to Dostoyevsky. In addition, while Dostoyevsky was writing *Crime and Punishment* there was a report of a Russian aristocrat who had been imprisoned for killing a man in a duel, and who had claimed that he deserved to be above the law. Thus, the Napoleonic theme in *Crime and Punishment* seems to have been developed by Dostoyevsky from similar themes expressed by other writers, as well as from actual events.

In addition to external sources for the novel's themes, there is evidence for external sources for many of the characters. Dostoyevsky himself was in constant financial trouble when writing the novel, and he actually borrowed a large sum of money from a senile elderly woman who was similar in many ways to the pawnbroker in the novel. Both women, for example, willed money to the church for prayers for their souls. Many lesser characters also seem to be drawn from people in Dostoyevsky's life, and in an early draft of the novel, one character is given the name of one of Dostoyevsky's creditors. Writings by Pushkin and Turgenev also provided Dostoyevsky with further sources for Raskolnikov.

In conclusion, there is evidence that many sources from Dostoyevsky's life contributed to the development of *Crime and Punishment*. Many authors had written on one of the two major themes and the other theme was at least partly related to Dostoyevsky's own experience in prison. In addition, a number of characters, including Raskolnikov, are related to individuals in Dostoyevsky's own life. In summary, this is another example of external sources providing at least some of the raw material with which the creative artist works.

Dostoyevsky is obviously not unique in such use of personal experiences in his writing. The novel *Tender is the Night* by F. Scott Fitzgerald closely follows many events in the author's life. In other cases, the influence is less direct, though still traceable. For example, the adventure stories of Robert Louis Stevenson are obviously not autobiographical; Stevenson never searched for Treasure Island, nor was he captured by pirates. In the Scottish Highlands where Stevenson grew up, however, stories were told of pirate adventures, and these stories served as raw material for Stevenson's novels. Although Stevenson did not experience these adventures directly, much information was available to him. Thus, even though an author may not have had certain experiences directly, one need not assume that an idea for a story comes to the author in a creative leap.

Development of a Painting

Because a painting hanging on a gallery wall is a single complete work, one tends to believe that it came about in a single act of creation. The unity of the completed work is deceptive, however, because much of the effort spent in painting cannot be seen on the finished canvas. The untrained observer seldom sees the changes made while work was in progress, changes which can greatly alter a work. Nor does the finished painting directly reflect such preparatory work as planning sketches or decisions about how the subject of the painting is to be arranged. This is true for any high-quality work of art; the finished product hides from the audience all preliminary work that went into it.

A number of different types of evidence are available, however, concerning the working procedures of artists, including several laboratory studies in which painters and poets were asked to work while being observed. Investigators have also studied the sketchbooks, notebooks, and original manuscripts of painters, writers, poets, and composers. In addition, there is at least one case in which a major artist, Pablo Picasso, kept a careful record of the preliminary work involved in the production of one of his major works, the mural *Guernica*. The evidence, which has been gathered from various sources, points to the same conclusion: works of art develop incrementally and the finished product usually is significantly different from the artist's original conception of it.

In laboratory investigations of the creative process, artists were given a subject to draw or paint. In one case a poem provided the inspiration; in another study the artist was given several objects to use as the basis for a still life.

In a study by Jan Eindhoven and Edgar Vinacke, artists and nonartists were asked to produce a picture to accompany the publication of a poem. The stimulus, an excerpt from a poem, was chosen because it was abstract and had no realistic or commonplace images. This presumably presented a problem to the subjects. The subjects were given white paper, drawing pencils, charcoal sticks, pen and ink, and black poster paint and brushes. No restrictions were placed on the subjects' use of the various media. The experimenter unobtrusively recorded several aspects of each session: the amount of time the subject spent reading the poem, time spent between reading the poem and beginning work, time spent working on a given picture, and time between pictures if more than one picture were done. In addition, the subject's progress and activity were recorded at five-minute intervals.

The study involved thirteen artists and a nonartist control group. The artists were all members of a professional association, in which membership was based on having a picture accepted for a jury show, and all derived some income from their art work. The nonartists were matched by age, race, sex, and I.Q.

This study presents some important, specific pieces of evidence about how artists work. Most subjects spent at least three sessions working on the project. The length of these sessions averaged more than thirty minutes, with the artists spending a bit more time in each session. One reason for the multiple sessions was that it took some time before the ultimate drawing was decided upon. In the first session, for example, all but one of the artists made more than one sketch, with an average production of almost four sketches. The nonartists produced fewer initial sketches; these were often little more than brief sketches of the primary characteristics of the picture (i.e., the general shape of the frame and the composition and gross outline of objects within the frame). Specific aspects of the final picture typically were added as the artist worked through a series of further sketches.

Most importantly, not only were the artists' final drawings larger and made from a wider variety of media than their initial drawings, they also differed in subject matter. Specifically, the final drawing often incorporated parts of earlier sketches though they were often significantly different from any one of them. The subject matter and composition of the initial drawings typically underwent changes as the artist worked through a series of sketches leading up to a final drawing.

In summary, this study reveals that drawings only gradually take shape as the artist works on the project. Although these results do not allow one to determine why an artist takes several sessions and a series of sketches to arrive at a final product, the pattern of results supports the view that the artist works through the problem in much the same way as has been discussed for other situations.

This emphasis on the evolution of a work of art is further supported by Jacob Getzels and Mihalyi Csikszentmihalyi, who asked thirty-one male students at the School of the Chicago Art Institute to draw a still life, while various aspects of their behavior were measured. The students were given many objects to use in the still life, including a woman's felt hat, a bunch of grapes, a prism, a trumpet, a book, a manikin, and a lens. Different types of drawing materials were available, and choice of subject matter and medium were left to the student. The investigators noted how many objects were manipulated, how unusual they were, and how carefully the student examined each one before beginning to draw. Once the student began to draw, a timed series of photographs was taken of the work in progress. This enabled the investigators to determine how much time elapsed from the beginning of drawing to the emergence of its final structure. The investigators also noted whether the student abandoned a drawing and started over, whether the arrangement of the objects was changed as the drawing progressed, and whether the final drawing simply copied the objects or represented them differently in some way.

Five art critics judged the drawings for quality, and several of the measured behaviors were found to be significantly related to the critics' judgments. The drawings rated most highly were produced by students who manipulated a greater number of objects before starting to draw, and who examined them most carefully. Highly rated pictures also tended to contain more unusual objects, nor were the objects simply copied. Getzels and Csikszentmihalyi also asked the students if they felt their final drawings were complete or if they could be improved in any way. The students who drew the highly rated pictures were more likely to report that further improvement was possible and that the drawing was not finished.

From the results found in this study, one can infer that a valuable product depends on relatively time-consuming work at the early stages. Such consideration, which may continue throughout the production of the work, contradicts the notion that artistic creations appear effortlessly in the mind of the artist. Although this conclusion came from an experimental situation in which the students were asked to draw, evidence shows that the results have wider generality. Getzels and Csikszentmihalyi conducted a follow-up study with these students seven years later. Members of the group had achieved varying degrees of success —some had left the art world altogether, others taught art but did not exhibit their own work, others did exhibit, and one had received notable success. Most interestingly, a number of the behaviors measured in the original drawing study were significantly related to the career success achieved by the students. The most successful artists tended to be those who had carefully examined a relatively large number of objects before starting to draw, who had taken a relatively long time before arriving at the final structure of their drawings, and who tended to restart their drawings and/or change the arrangement of objects as they worked. Apparently, therefore, the tendency toward critical analysis before and during work was important in the success of the drawings produced in the original study and in the career success of these artists as well.

From these results, one might conclude that the successful artist approaches all work with a high set of standards, both in determining what the work will contain and in judging how well the planned work is executed. Furthermore, one cannot break this critical analysis down into neat stages of planning then execution because the successful artist is ready to modify the structure of a work even when it is far along in its execution. The better students in the Getzels and Csikszentmihalyi study indicated that their drawings could have been improved further, even after they had stopped working on them. Critical analysis is thus an integral aspect of artistic creation, from the very beginning of a project to the point when the artist decides to stop working, although more critical analysis and modification could still be done.

Further evidence for the idea that works of art gradually evolve and that the artist's constant critical analysis is important in that evolution is found in the work of Pablo Picasso.

Fig. 7.2
Pablo Picasso, *Guernica.* (Padro, Madrid. Copyright SPADEM/VAGA, New York, 1986.)

On April 26, 1937, during the Spanish civil war, the Nazi air force, allied with Francisco Franco, the leader of the Spanish fascists, attacked and almost completely destroyed the Spanish town of Guernica. The town was not important militarily, but it had played an important role in the history of Spain for over 600 years, especially in the history of the Basque people. The destruction of the town and the massacre of civilians, therefore, were highly symbolic, making the brutality of Franco and his Nazi allies vividly clear.

The bombing of Guernica served as the stimulus for the creation of a major work by Picasso. In January, 1937, the Spanish government commissioned Picasso to paint a mural for its building at the Paris World's Fair. Picasso deeply hated the Spanish fascists who were winning the civil war and he carried out his commission by painting a mural that depicted the bombing of Guernica. This painting has become a universal statement on the horrors of war. To students of artistic creativity, *Guernica* has additional importance because Picasso retained and catalogued all preliminary work on the mural, which involves some forty works of various sorts. Photographs were also taken of the mural in various stages of completion. This information is extremely useful in tracing the development of the painting as the artist worked on it.

The mural, presented in Figure 7.2, contains nine "characters" of various sorts: a bull at the far left stands over a mother holding a dead child, a bird flies upward toward the "sun" in the center, a horse in the center screams in agony, a statute of a warrior holding a sword lies in pieces along the bottom, a woman in the upper center looks out of a window while holding a light, a "fugitive" woman is in the lower right, and a falling woman is in the upper right.

As mentioned earlier, a finished work of art hides its development from the naive observer, but Picasso's presentation and cataloguing of his preliminary work makes available much interesting information about the development of *Guernica.* Of the forty-odd preliminary drawings, seven are composition studies in which something like the entire mural is presented with varying degrees of specificity. Several of these compositional studies are shown in Figure 7.3, and

Fig. 7.3
Pablo Picasso, composition studies for *Guernica*. (Prado, Madrid. Copyright SPADEM/VAGA, New York, 1986.)

from them one can get a sense of the painting's direction and development. One striking aspect of these compositional studies is the relatively large changes that occur from one to the next. For example, the bull, perhaps the most important character in the final mural, is not even present in some of the sketches, and its position and attitude vary greatly from study to study when it is present. The same is true of the horse, the warrior, and the mother and child. Characters are introduced and removed, large positional changes occur, and so on. Furthermore, the development in this series of compositional studies does not move in one consistent direction, as it might have had Picasso begun with one general idea and merely refined it as he worked. On the contrary, the compositional studies reveal that Picasso tried several different possibilities that were not directly related to each other, although many similarities existed between them. Furthermore, the first version on canvas was very different from the final version, indicating that Picasso began to paint without having a final version of the mural in mind.

In addition to the compositional studies, Picasso also kept the studies he made of the individual characters in the mural. Each main character was examined in several variations, in sketches and in the mural itself, before reaching its final form. Some evidence of this can be seen in the composition studies shown in Figure 7.3 in which the bull and the horse undergo multiple changes. Additional changes occur in the other preliminary work. For example, the horse appears in twelve preliminary studies, ranging from realistic drawings of the animal in agony to a child-like drawing of an emotionless standing horse. Furthermore, the horse changes considerably in the pictures taken of the mural in progress.

The mother and child also appear in various forms in approximately ten preliminary studies. Likewise, the bull appears in five separate studies in which its appearance varies greatly, particularly its head. The bull's orientation in the final version of the mural differs from its orientation in the first version and from those in the compositional studies in Figure 7.3. The warrior, introduced in a compositional study as one of many fallen human beings at the bottom of the mural, is changed considerably in position throughout Picasso's working on the mural until he becomes a broken statue in the final version. In addition to the modification of final elements, a number of components in early versions of the mural were later removed by Picasso and do not appear in the final version.

Conclusions   Picasso's method of working, as exemplified in the preliminary sketches and the photographs of the mural in various stages of completion, is strikingly similar to the methods found by Eindhoven and Vinacke and by Getzels and Csikszentmihalyi in their laboratory studies of artists. The evidence for detailed critical analysis is visible in Picasso's work, both before the mural was begun and while it was being painted. Several possibilities for the general composition of the mural were considered before Picasso began to paint, and the composition underwent further changes while he painted. Likewise, specific aspects of the characters were considered again and again in preliminary work and then modified still further as the painting progressed.

In examining the preparatory work for *Guernica,* one gets the feeling that Picasso is very hard to satisfy and always ready to try once more to get some small detail a little better. There is one interesting difference between Picasso's critical analysis of his work and that of the art students examined by Getzels and Csikszentmihalyi. The best students tended to feel that their "finished" work could have been further improved. Supposedly, when Picasso finished working on a painting, he was through with it and he went on to the next one. His critical analysis ended when the work reached a stage which he considered completion. The importance of this difference is unclear, but it should not detract from the extensive critical analysis that went into Picasso's work, as is exemplified by his work on *Guernica.*

Sources for Guernica

As our analysis shows, Picasso's preliminary work on *Guernica* demonstrates that the painting did not come to him as a unified work but rather developed as he continuously tried out various ideas, and variations on these ideas, until something at last satisfied him. Assuming that Picasso worked hard to bring *Guernica* to its final state, however, there is still the question of why he chose to paint what he did. Why did his early studies contain certain elements and not others? This question is a very complex one, and before attempting to answer it, I want to make it clear that certain answers are beyond the scope of this discussion. One might attempt to answer the question of Picasso's choice of characters with psychoanalysis and by interpreting the unconscious symbolism in the bull, the horse, the various female figures, and so on. Such in-depth analysis is not intended here, nor am I qualified to psychoanalyze Picasso. I am more interested in the surface history of the various forms, that is, how these various forms appeared in Picasso's earlier work and in the work of others with which he was fa-

Fig. 7.4
Pablo Picasso, *Minotauromachy*. (Philadelphia Museum of Art: Given by
Henry P. McIlhenny.)

miliar. Despite the fact that *Guernica* looks very "modern" and different from
anything painted before, I hope to show that by examining Picasso's work and
his interest in the work of others, one can see at least broadly where *Guernica*
came from.

The characters that appear in *Guernica* also appeared in many of Picasso's
earlier works. Picasso's earlier etching, *Minotauromachy* (Figure 7.4), contains
many similar characters, although the overall theme is very different. *Minotauromachy* contains a bull (or a variation on a bull), a suffering horse with a raised
head, a dead human figure clutching a sword, a female holding a light, a woman
looking out of a window located at the corner of a building, birds, and a vertical
human figure along the border. In addition, the positioning of the characters in
Minotauromachy is particularly intriguing when one considers how an etching is
made. The artist first transfers the scene to a printing plate, which is then used
to print the image on paper. When the image is printed, the left-to-right relationships among objects on the plate is reversed. That is, if we put objects in lo-
cations A-B-C on a printing plate, the printed image on the paper will appear
C-B-A. Thus, when Picasso put *Minotauromachy* on the printing plate, the bull
was drawn on the left and the building with its windows, the vertical person, the
horse, and the dead human were all located in the positions they hold in *Guernica*. The characters and organization of *Guernica*, therefore, seem to be a variation on things Picasso did before, not something completely new.

It should also be emphasized that many of these characters appear again and
again in Picasso's work, before (and after) *Guernica*. A dominant bull and a suf-

fering horse, for example, are portrayed together many times in Picasso's drawings and paintings of bullfights. The dead baby's head, which falls completely backwards until it is upside-down, is directly related to a 1929 work in which a human head appears in the same position. As this brief analysis indicates, *Guernica* was by no means a novel event in Picasso's career.

There is also evidence that *Guernica* was not a novel event in the history of painting. Anthony Blunt's provocative analysis of *Guernica's* place in art history points out many connections between Picasso's work and that of earlier artists. First of all, the use of a bull as a symbol dates back to at least Minoan civilization (3500–1400 BC). Many of Picasso's other characters, and the way he represented them, also have deep roots in European art. Blunt traces the overall organization of *Guernica,* in which much of the emotion is portrayed through women, to a long series of paintings by sixteenth and seventeenth century artists who portrayed *The Massacre of the Innocents,* the slaughter of children by soldiers hoping to kill the infant Jesus. In addition, Blunt traces specific figures in *Guernica* to influences from earlier works. One such possible influence is shown in Figure 7.5. As can be seen, the resemblance between the woman in this painting and the woman in *Guernica* is striking. Blunt also believes that Picasso's choice of the mother holding her dead baby, and his way of presenting them, stem from his knowledge of the importance of such figures in earlier masterpieces.

Blunt also finds a surprising source for some of the other characters in the mural. The warrior statue at the bottom of the mural, for example, bears a striking resemblance to a figure in an illustration from an eleventh century Spanish manuscript of the Apocalypse (Figure 7.6). A related manuscript also contains figures of women whose eyes both appear on the same side of the nose, a characteristic of the women in *Guernica.* The Apocalypse manuscript also contains symbols for the four Evangelists; at least one of these symbols is very similar to one of Picasso's studies for the bull in *Guernica.* Furthermore, Blunt's analysis is made plausible by evidence that Picasso was familiar with these various manuscripts.

In conclusion, Blunt's analysis supports the view that *Guernica* bears traces of other influences—from Picasso's earlier work as well as that by other artists. In one sense, these wide influences make Picasso's work even more impressive, because they are evidence of Picasso's deep knowledge of art.

Development of a Symphony

One of the most valuable sources of information concerning the role of early work in artistic production is found in the musical sketchbooks left by Ludwig van Beethoven. These books contain over 5000 pages of preliminary material, and they make graphically clear the large amount of energy Beethoven expended in refining an idea over and over until he was either satisfied with it or cast it aside. The Ninth Symphony is a good example of the composer's extensive reworking of a piece. The Ninth Symphony is the final symphony Beethoven wrote, and it is the first such work by any composer to include the human voice as an integral part. (The last movement includes Frederick Schiller's

Fig. 7.5
J.-A.-D. Ingres, study for *The Martyrdom of St. Symphorian*, detail.
(Courtesy of the Fogg Art Museum, Harvard University, Grenville L.
Winthrop Bequest.)

poem, "Ode to Joy.") Like all such "revolutionary" advances, Beethoven's earlier work anticipated this in two ways. First, his 1808 *Choral Fantasy* used a
chorus in an orchestral piece, though the piece was not a symphony. Second,
Beethoven had had the "Ode to Joy" in mind as the basis for a composition for a
long time. The Ninth Symphony was completed in 1824, but Beethoven had
first thought about setting the "Ode to Joy" to music thirty-one years earlier,
and in 1812 he had considered writing still another piece based on it.

In 1817, and perhaps even as early as 1815, one finds the first sketches that
can be directly related to the final version of the Ninth, though the elaboration
of these sketches did not take place until 1822 or 1823. The Ninth Symphony
did not contain a choral finale in its initial form. Beethoven originally contemplated two symphonies, his Ninth and Tenth, and the choral movement was intended as the finale of the latter. It was when he merged the two symphonies
into one, that the Ninth acquired the choral finale. The merger raised concerns
about whether the earlier movements and the finale would fit together, however, and the sketchbooks are proof of the extensive work Beethoven did before
he was satisfied that the various parts belonged together. This is a very impor-

Fig. 7.6
Apocalypse, Spanish, eleventh century, detail. (Bibliothèque Nationale, Paris.)

tant piece of information, given Beethoven's reputation for the "organic" nature of his work as it relates to the unity and cohesion of the various parts of even long pieces. Beethoven's notebooks indicate that this cohesion is the result of his efforts to take separate ideas and make them unified. Obviously, the "organic unity" of the completed Ninth did not exist initially since the parts came from sketches for separate works.

Thus, Beethoven's Ninth Symphony is another example of a work which neither came to the artist whole, nor unfolded simply from one or a few germinal ideas. Rather, several ideas that had been under consideration for many years gradually came together to result in the symphony as it is known today, but this "coming together" required a great deal of work. The Ninth Symphony is by no means an isolated example of such extensive revision in Beethoven's work. If one examines his other eight symphonies, one sees many examples of works started, put aside, and later returned to; of works in which parts were dropped after much elaboration; and of works in which a small phrase or idea was returned to again and again until it finally emerged as something very different. Nor is Beethoven's revisionist technique limited to his symphonic writing—his sketchbooks contain *thirteen* versions of one aria included in his opera *Fidelio*.

In conclusion, this great composer was also one of the all-time great revisers. Although he may have been unique among composers in his obsessive concern with revision, he was by no means unique in his use of revision. Early drafts of musical compositions left behind by many composers show evidence of revision as well as evidence of works being begun and dropped. These findings parallel those already discussed.

Sources of New Ideas in Music: The Composer as Borrower

As with poetry, literature, and painting, it is also possible to trace the sources of musical works. Analyses of the works of the greatest composers has revealed many sources. My discussion begins with the work of Johann Sebastian Bach, one of the most prolific composers.

Bach was born in central Germany into a family of musicians. His father and uncles were musicians, and the Bach family had supplied musicians to churches and town bands in the area for over 100 years. Orphaned at age ten, Bach was raised by an older brother who was an organist. In his two marriages, Bach fathered twenty children; ten died in infancy, one died in his twenties, and one was retarded. Of the surviving eight, three became leading composers of the next generation.

Bach's professional life was spent in the direct service of others, and he composed and performed music as a requirement of his work. He obtained his first position at age eighteen as church organist at Arnstadt. At twenty-three he received his first important post as court organist and chamber musician to the Duke of Weimar. During the nine years he held this post he produced many great works for the organ. In 1717, the Duke refused to advance Bach in rank and Bach accepted an offer from the Prince of Anholt-Cöthen. The Duke of Weimar would not release Bach from his service, however, and Bach spent some time in jail for refusing to work, until the Duke got disgusted enough to release him from his service. At Cöthen, Bach wrote much chamber music for the entertainment of the Prince and his guests.

In 1723, Bach was appointed Cantor of St. Thomas Church in Leipzig, which was one of the most important musical posts in Germany. Interestingly, he was the third choice for the post, one reason being that he did not have extensive experience in writing the sort of music the position required. There were at least two other musicians in the area with far greater reputations than Bach's. Bach's duties as cantor were many and varied: he taught at the choir school and gave the choirboys lessons in Latin; in addition, he served as music director, composer, organist, and choirmaster of the church. Bach remained at Leipzig from 1723 until his death in 1750.

The various positions Bach held made strong demands on his compositional skills. Music was an integral part of the Lutheran Sunday service, and the cantor was expected to write much of it. Bach wrote many cantatas (sacred texts set to music) for the Sunday services at Leipzig. At least one cantata was needed for each week of the year and additional ones were needed for holidays, so that approximately 60 cantatas were needed for a yearly cycle. Bach composed five cycles of cantatas (about 300 cantatas) while at Leipzig, of which approximately 200 are presently known. Thus, one direct stimulus to Bach's productivity was the demands his position placed on him. A professional musician under contract to a patron or institution was expected to be almost continuously productive.

It is important to note in this context that the present-day interest in "old" music is a comparatively new phenomenon. Throughout the seventeenth and eighteenth centuries audiences were interested only in new music, and composers were kept busy producing new pieces for their next performance. The idea of a composer producing something to meet his or her own private creative needs, rather than public demands, is relatively new and was unknown to someone like Bach.

Of course, this still leaves a further question: How did the composer meet these demands for productivity? One possibility is that Bach and others like him simply were constantly inspired and produced an unending flow of new and valuable music. It is difficult to conceive of Bach constantly producing new works, however, especially with all the additional responsibilities, both professional and familial, he carried out. Since Bach and other prolific composers were not superhuman, how did they produce the music they were constantly in need of? For Bach and the other composers of his era there were several ways in which composition was made more manageable.

The rules of composition, first of all, specified the musical structure of various sorts of compositions. The baroque fugue, for example, was written according to precise rules which specified how themes were to be used, what sorts of repetitions should occur, and so on. There were also guidelines for relating music to words, especially important to composers of church music. These guidelines were based on rhetoric, the ancient art of speaking whereby orators were instructed in the use of different figures of speech. These figures were used to elaborate the oration in such a way as to maximize the emotional impact on the audience. In the seventeenth and eighteenth centuries, rhetorical concepts were adapted to the art of writing music, and certain musical forms were customarily used to express various aspects of the meaning of the text the composer was setting to music. Thus, the composer did not have to begin anew each time a new text was to be set to music. These rhetorical guidelines presented an outline for the composition to take. Although they might not be strictly adhered to, they served to at least somewhat relieve the composer's inspirational burden.

A second device to ease the composer's burden was the practice of borrowing musical ideas, from oneself and from others. A composer would often use an old melody as the basis for a new piece or perhaps adopt the composition of another composer for personal use. Bach often borrowed from himself and from others. Norman Carrell has attempted to trace every instance of such borrowing, and his conclusions are of great interest to students of creative thinking. Over 225 of Bach's nonvocal works contain borrowings from his own earlier works. In his nonvocal works, Carrell traces more than eighty cases of borrowing from other composers, perhaps the most famous of which are the transcriptions for harpsichord of several of Antonio Vivaldi's violin concertos. Carrell finds Vivaldi's influence in much of Bach's work, and believes that Bach owed Vivaldi much in the way of inspiration, in addition to the works which are based directly on Vivaldi's compositions.

Bach's vocal works, including the cycles of cantatas, also depended heavily on borrowing. Carrell estimates that approximately 65 percent of the presently known cantatas contain borrowings from Bach's own works. In addition, the cantatas also depend heavily on Lutheran hymns and over 200 of them contain a hymn melody as the basis for a chorale, or choral setting of the hymn, in the last section of the cantata. Some cantatas use the hymn melody in several sections in addition to the chorale.

In summary, one of the ways Bach met the seemingly superhuman demands of his positions was through the very human device of revising something old to fit the new demand. Such borrowing, however, was not considered plagiarism. Using someone else's or one's own earlier work as the starting point for a new composition was accepted musical practice then. Furthermore, Bach's use of borrowed material usually involved such elaboration and extension that an essentially new composition was produced. Indeed, one aspect of Bach's genius was his ability to borrow a piece from another and turn it into something immeasurably finer. Also, it is important to remember that though Bach did not create something new each time, perhaps no one else could have done what he did with the ideas of others or could have produced the original ideas that he did produce.

It is important to emphasize that such borrowing did not make Bach unique in any way. Another acknowledged master of the baroque era, George Frederick Handel, also is well known for his extensive reuse of his own works and his borrowing from others. As an example of the former, Handel's famous *Music for the Royal Fireworks,* first performed in 1749 to celebrate a peace treaty, contains music that he had used at least twice before. In addition, several of his oratorios contain complete movements taken from the works of others, and various instrumental pieces are based directly on other composers' writings, among them Georg Philipp Telemann, whose music Handel is known to have studied carefully. Handel's habit of borrowing from other composers was so well known that a number of his contemporaries mentioned it in public articles and private letters. In addition to such explicit borrowing, Handel is also believed to have significantly changed his style of composition in response to the success of a rival composer, Giovanni Buononcini, making his works simpler, more melodious, and more "singable" in imitation of the other's style.

The same pattern is also seen in other composers. Mozart, for example, participated in a musical competition with Muzio Clementi (1752–1832) in 1781, in which he, Mozart, was generally acknowledged to be the superior performer. Though Mozart dismissed Clementi afterward as mechanical, without taste or feeling, this low opinion did not prevent him from using as the basis of one of his own pieces a melody played by Clementi at the competition.

Many composers have written pieces that are variations on a theme by another composer, such as Brahms's *Variations on a Theme by Haydn,* and Beethoven's *Diabelli Variations.* Beethoven also used his own material several times, as with the dance that serves as the basis for the finale of the *Eroica Symphony.* This piece is one of a set of twelve dances and it was also used as the basis for a set of variations. Interestingly, recent arguments claim that a theme by Carl Phillip Emanuel Bach, which Beethoven knew well, is the source of this dance. Beethoven never acknowledged using Bach's theme, but Elwood Derr presents evidence that much of Beethoven's inspiration concerning this piece came from the music of C.P.E. Bach.

The importance of folk melodies and folk dances in classical composition also must be emphasized. Many works in the baroque and classical eras, such as baroque dance suites and the movements of many classical symphonies, were based directly on folk forms. In addition, the European folk melodies formed a tradition from which composers of the seventeenth and eighteenth centuries constantly drew inspiration. One musicologist estimates that 80 percent of Mozart's melodies also appeared in the compositions of his contemporaries, indicating a common use of sources. Many composers in different eras have taken folk melodies and used them as the basis for compositions, such as Dvorak's *Slavonic Dances,* Brahms's *Hungarian Dances,* and works by Bartok, Liszt, Chopin, Mozart, Beethoven, Orff, and many others.

In conclusion, much musical composition can be identified as the direct reworking of earlier ideas, either those of the composer in question or those of other composers. This is not to say that musical creativity is not involved, but simply that creation never occurs in a vacuum. One would be surprised indeed if no traces of earlier influences existed. Though these traces may be more or less explicit, depending on the circumstances, they are invariably present.

Learning to Create

I believe one point should be strongly emphasized, and that is that artistic creation is a skill that must be learned. Poets, painters, novelists, playwrights, composers, and sculptors all undergo extended periods of formal or informal training before they are capable of producing something that others value. Composers, for example, are not born with the ability to write great music; they acquire it through teaching and practice and, with practice, their skill improves. The musical compositions we are familiar with are written by *professionals,* by individuals who have studied and worked for years before their skills developed sufficiently to enable them to express something musically. Though it is right that we lose sight of the preparatory work involved when we listen to a great piece of music, to understand the processes involved in its creation, it is imperative that we have some idea of the arduous training involved.

A recent study by John Hayes provides strong evidence for the importance of practice in learning to compose. Hayes began with some recent psychological research on expertise in problem solving, including expertise in chess playing. The research concluded that more than ten years of training, study, and practice are needed before one reaches a "creative" level of problem solving. This led Hayes to wonder if comparable experience was necessary to achieve eminence in the arts, specifically in music.

In order to answer this question, Hayes first analyzed the compositions of Mozart. Mozart began studying music at age four and produced his first symphony at age eight—if any individual were exceptional enough to need little or no training or experience before producing great works, Mozart would be the one. Hayes attempted to define the quality of individual pieces of Mozart's work by how many recordings of it were available. Hayes reasoned that the presence of many recordings reflects a consensus among the musical establishment (what performers wish to record), the recording industry (what they believe will sell), and public taste (what people ultimately buy). On examining *Schwann's Record and Tape Guide,* a listing of all available recordings, Hayes found that Mozart's early works are not well represented on records. Although 12 percent of Mozart's works were composed in the first ten years of his career, only 5 percent of the available recordings come from this period. Furthermore, many of these early works are included in collections, such as the complete symphonies of Mozart, which led Hayes to surmise that they were included more for completeness of the collection than for their inherent quality. Hayes then defined a "masterwork" as one for which five different recordings were available in the catalogue, and by that definition, Mozart wrote his first masterwork in the 12th year of his career. Based on this analysis, Hayes concluded that Mozart's early works were of lower quality than were his later works. This is also the opinion of music critics. Thus, even Mozart needed to learn to compose.

Hayes extended his catalogue method to examine the masterwork production of seventy-six of the composers discussed in Harold Schonberg's *Lives of the Great Composers,* for whom enough information was available to determine when they began to study music. Of these seventy-six composers, only three produced masterworks after fewer than ten years of musical preparation. Hayes found that the production of masterworks by his definition depended on the number of years the composer had prepared, not simply on his or her absolute age. That is, composers who started in music relatively late in life took at least as long to produce a masterwork as did those who started much earlier, indicating that the younger composers were not simply "maturing," but were developing some rather specific musical skills. Given Hayes's intriguing results, which have strong implications for the role of specific learning experiences in musical composition, it now becomes interesting to consider what the education of a composer typically entails.

The biographical notes on the jackets of classical records often include something about when and with whom the composer studied, though the information is rarely explicit. Upon examining more detailed biographies, one finds some common methods to which all student composers were, and still are, subjected. One of the most important methods is the immersion of the composer-to-be in the music of earlier composers. This immersion entails very detailed study of the works of others, down to the young musician's copying the works of others into notebooks. The works of others are performed until they are known thoroughly, and the young composer practices by composing in the style of others. Several composers have left behind notebooks containing these transcriptions and their primitive attempts to compose in this way. One commentator even suggested that Handel's habit of borrowing may have originated in his early training of copying the works of others.

A second important aspect of musical training involves learning certain rules of composition. These rules changed somewhat as music evolved over the centuries, but certain central notions have been present for at least 300 years. Students are taught rules of harmony, which involve learning what sorts of sequences of chords are permissible and what sorts of melody notes go with which chords. Interestingly, even relatively modern books on harmony refer to Bach for examples, indicating an underlying continuity despite the great surface changes that have occurred since Bach's time. Thus, these basic building blocks enable composers to take the first steps of composing. These tools are just a foundation, of course, since each musical era has its own forms that go beyond the basics. It goes without saying that each composer brings his or her individual capacities to the enterprise of making music. That is, each person uses what he or she has learned and goes further with it differently. The important point, however, is that in the beginning even the greatest musical geniuses did little more than copy or imitate the great works of others.

Summary

This chapter provided evidence for the incremental nature of creative thinking in the arts, by demonstrating that innovation in art is firmly grounded in earlier work, both that of other artists and of the artist in question; that innovation occurs as the initial product evolves into something new; and that this innovation occurs in a series of small steps rather than a great leap. The discussion first centered on large-scale innovation, as when a new style or kind of work is developed, such as Calder's mobiles and the collages of Braque and Picasso. In both cases, the evolutionary nature of the innovation was apparent because these new forms developed from earlier interests and work of the artists. The development of a single work was then considered in the discussion of Picasso's mural *Guernica*. It was found that a single work of art also evolves as the artist revises earlier work until something novel and satisfying is produced. Similar conclusions were drawn from discussions of work in poetry, music, and literature. Finally, evidence revealed that the initial ideas an artist uses as the basis for the evolution of a new work come from his or her earlier work or that of other artists.

The view presented in this chapter is very similar to the views of artistic creativity proposed by art scholars. As an example, Anthony Blunt, the well-known art historian and critic, whose analysis of *Guernica* has already been discussed in detail, has this comment about the apparent creative leaps in Picasso's work.

> [W]e are told that Picasso changes his style so frequently and so rapidly that no one would realize that works of different periods were by the same artist. But what art historian—if he did not know the intervening stages—could guess that early and late works by Titian, Rembrandt, Poussin, or Cézanne were by the same hand? And if, with Picasso, one carries out the process of following through the intervening stages, it becomes apparent that, although the first and last productions of his imagination are widely separated—even fundamentally different—the change was brought about by a series of steps, each of which is intelligible and can be seen as following logically on the earlier moves, and each of which was arrived at by a process of experiment and thought . . . .

As one can see, Blunt's opinion agrees with the view presented here. The fact that his conclusion is drawn from a career of study of artists indicates that an incremental perspective may have very wide relevance.

In conclusion, the analyses of artistic creativity in this chapter support those concerning scientific creativity developed in the last chapter. When detailed information was present, incremental evolution of creative products rather than insightful leaps was the rule in all the cases analyzed. Though only a very limited number of cases were analyzed, these involved scientists and artists of the very highest level of genius. Therefore, if creative leaps are not found here, it is doubtful whether they will be found anywhere.

8

THE INCREMENTAL NATURE OF CREATIVITY: SOME BROADER ISSUES

The point of view presented in Chapter 1 has now been elaborated in a number of ways. A critical analysis of various aspects of the "genius" view of creativity has raised doubts about whether human creativity is a mysterious phenomenon involving extraordinary thought processes and extraordinary individuals. The results of this critical analysis indicate that many of the traditional beliefs are poorly supported by hard evidence. No evidence was found for the role of unconscious processes in creative thinking, for example, except in the subjective reports of scientists and artists, which are of questionable value as evidence. Laboratory studies have produced no evidence for incubation and illumination, phenomena presumed to depend on unconscious thought processes.

In the same way, little support was found for the notion that creative problem solving occurs in a leap of insight (an "aha!" experience) as the problem solver breaks out of the fixation resulting from his or her past experience. Such "aha!" experiences have been extremely difficult to bring about in the laboratory, even when the alleged fixation was broken. Furthermore, evidence from research studies indicates that, rather than being independent of past experience, solution of "insight" problems depends on detailed past experience with such problems. Little support was found for the related view that creativity depends on divergent thinking, which supposedly is fostered by the brainstorming technique. This method, which involves the production of ideas without judgment of their adequacy, has been advocated as a method of increasing creative problem solving by those who believe that many varied ideas are necessary in order for creative problem solving to occur. In the brainstorming method, judgment is only brought into play after ideas are generated. Research indicates that judgment is crucial in creative thinking from the very beginning, however, not solely after ideas are generated. As discussed in Chapter 4, the postulation of divergent thinking as a crucial factor in creative thinking may be due to a mistaken analogy drawn from the difference between what happens when we observe someone else solve a problem and when we try to solve a problem ourselves. Finally, evidence indicates that the creative individual does not derive this capacity from a set of unique personality characteristics. To the degree that they are valid, these analyses support the conclusion that the traditional view of creative thinking is incorrect and that we need a different way of dealing with creative thinking.

In addition to these negative conclusions, Chapters 6 and 7 analyzed examples of high-quality creative thinking in the sciences and the arts in order to provide further support for the incremental view presented in Chapter 1. This view assumes that all creative acts are firmly grounded in the work of other individuals, as well as the work of the individual in question. The creative product comes about as a result of modification and elaboration of earlier work; and the new product evolves in a series of small steps as the thinker moves slowly away from earlier work. This view of creative thinking was proposed on the basis of evidence from laboratory studies of undergraduates solving simple problems, as well as studies of the role of expertise in problem solving in several domains. The analyses in Chapters 6 and 7 further support the generality of these ideas.

In Chapter 6, two historic scientific discoveries were considered—Darwin's discovery of evolution through natural selection and Watson and Crick's discovery of the double helix of DNA. In both of these discoveries, the scientists' interest in the problem and their initial methods of attacking it were related to their individual backgrounds. Also, in both cases, initial methods had to be modified as deficiencies became apparent. Finally, these modifications occurred in small steps as new information, which became available as the scientists worked on the problems, made it clear that various aspects of the initial proposal were inadequate.

In Chapter 7, the incremental view was applied to creativity in the arts. Innovation in art was considered on a broad scale, as when an artist produces a new style of work, such as Calder's development of mobiles; and on a narrower scale, as when an artist produces a single new work in the context of a whole career, such as Picasso's mural *Guernica.* On the broad scale, it was found that a new style develops gradually as the interests of the artist interact with various life experiences. In the case of Calder's development of mobiles, his early interest in metal sculpture and in movement interacted with his exposure to the circus, to moving animal music boxes, and to Mondrian's abstract style of painting. These various streams came together to produce the mobiles we are familiar with today. On the narrower scale, analysis of *Guernica* indicated that a strong relationship existed between various aspects of that work and earlier work, both by Picasso and by other artists. These are only two of several cases presented to support the view that artistic creativity is also incremental in nature.

It is now possible to examine a number of broader issues that could not be considered until the detailed information contained in these earlier chapters was presented. First, I examine the multifaceted nature of creative thinking and provide further support for the notion that no small set of psychological processes is constant in all creative acts. Second, I consider in greater detail whether there really are no differences between creative geniuses and other individuals, as far as thinking processes and personality characteristics are concerned. Because the discussion in Chapters 6 and 7 provided further information about such individuals, the analysis here can be more specific than it was in Chapter 5. Finally, I reconsider some of the assumptions underlying the genius view of creativity in order to discuss the most useful way to analyze the relationship between "creative" and "ordinary" thinking. This analysis results in a change of perspective that eliminates much of the mystery surrounding creative thinking.

The Multiple Facets of Creative Thinking

The discussion in Chapter 1 of creative problem solving provided a framework for the analysis of a broad range of phenomena, though little attempt was made to define creative thinking explicitly. (It was assumed that our intuitive understanding of that concept was enough.) Based on the discussion in Chapters 2 through 7, however, more can now be said about creative thinking of various sorts. The claim was made in the earlier discussion that different types of situations call forth different types of thinking processes, and that the thought processes involved in creative thinking are no different than those involved in more ordinary activities. The present discussion considers these claims further and examines some of the many different ways creative thinking can be exhibited, even within the single domain of what may be called "problem solving." As will be seen, the thought processes involved in these situations are also involved in other "noncreative" situations.

A creative solution to a problem must meet two criteria: it must be novel and it must solve the problem in question. The criterion of novelty has already been discussed in detail in a number of places and needs no further discussion here. The second criterion, adequate solution of the problem, bears further elaboration because problems come in at least two types and the adequacy of solution is defined differently in each. In *well-defined* problems, the characteristics of the solution are specified precisely at the beginning, so that the problem solver knows which criteria the solution must meet. An example of a well-defined problem is tic-tac-toe, in which the types of solutions are specified exactly by rules known to both players.

In an *ill-defined* problem, on the other hand, a detailed specification of the goal is not part of the problem itself. In such a problem, the problem solver must specify in some detail the criteria that the solution must meet. Examples of ill-defined problems are deciding on a career and choosing how to spend one's vacation. The candle problem, discussed in Chapter 1, is ill-defined since the only criteria given to the problem solver are that the candle be up on the wall and that it burn properly. Nothing in the problem tells the problem solver exactly what "burn properly" means, forcing the individual to supply such specific criteria as whether the candle must be vertical, whether wax can drip on the table, and so forth.

The distinction between well- and ill-defined problems will help to provide a framework for the analysis of several situations involving creative thinking, both in the specific area of problem solving and in other areas.

In Chapter 1, I described an incident in which I used a quarter to cover the end of a pipe in my car's engine. I initially thought of cutting a circle from cardboard, but questions of its strength led to the idea of a metal disc, although fabricating one entailed further problems. At just this time I had to pay a toll, and the quarter came to mind as an already-made metal disc.

Assuming that my recollection of this incident is reasonably accurate, a number of different sorts of processes are important here. First, this is an ill-defined problem, since the form of the solution is not specified. The decision to start with a cardboard circle came from me, through a relatively straightforward retrieval of information from memory: if one needs something, one tries to make it; and a simple way of making a small circle is out of cardboard. The realization that the cardboard might collapse, however, was based on the use of knowledge and imagination. That is, I imagined (visualized) a cardboard disc in place, and saw (realized) that it might not withstand the pressure. The ability to carry out this reasoning was based on experience with cardboard, that is, I could bring my knowledge about cardboard's strength to the situation. The thought of a metal disc then came about through retrieval of additional information from memory: if one thing collapses, try something stronger. Obviously, these processes are used used by everyone all the time.

Thus, at the risk of oversimplification, one could speculate that the novel use of my quarter came about through basically perceptual processes, that is, my knowledge of the sensory characteristics of cardboard was used as the basis for a perceptual analysis of how cardboard might perform. This perceptually based reasoning process was made up of retrieving information from memory, using this information as the basis for imagining a solution to the problem, and then estimating whether or not this solution would work. Although this may not be reasoning in the true sense of using logical formulas and formal rules of inference, it may be analogous to such reasoning.

The candle problem is also an ill-defined problem, and its solution begins with the retrieval of information from memory concerning how one attaches things in general, or candles in particular, to walls. This retrieval process results in the problem solver setting criteria for the solution. As discussed in Chapter 1, solving the problem by using the box to hold the candle came about through the problem solver's perceptually-based estimation of the inadequacy of other solutions, such as gluing the candle to the wall. These estimations involved such processes as estimating the strength of the adhesive needed to hold the candle and were based on past experience with glue and the like. Again, perceptual imagination played a role.

Thus, the processes involved in the candle problem may have been quite similar to those just discussed concerning the novel use of a quarter: retrieval of perceptual information from memory, and use of this information to imagine the consequences of carrying out possible solutions.

The Charlie problem involved the subject's deducing that Charlie was a fish which died when his bowl was knocked over and broken by Tom, a cat. This problem is also ill-defined, since one is told neither exactly how Charlie died nor all the circumstances surrounding his death. Individuals begin to solve the problem by recalling ways in which people can die based on what the problem seems to ask for. The solution to this problem may involve more than the perceptual information discussed so far, since it depends on verbal concepts and whether or not the questions based on these concepts produce reasonable answers. For example, when an individual tries to specify Charlie's age and finds that Charlie is a year old but is not an infant, one's definition of an infant is contradicted. This in turn leads to the retrieval of a concept that fits the facts, that is, that Charlie is not human. Thus, verbal concepts may play a more important role in this problem than in the others discussed so far. Again, however, we all possess such concepts (we all know what words mean) and we are all capable of determining whether or not such concepts are being used correctly, as when we correct the speech of others.

Another example of an ill-defined problem is the state Watson and Crick were in when they began work on the structure of DNA. Though they began with some general information about DNA's structure and function, they knew nothing about the precise form of the structure. Watson and Crick decided to use the helix as the basis for their work, that is, they adopted that aspect of the solution when they began working on the problem.

The discovery of the double helix began with a straightforward retrieval of information from memory. Faced with the problem of determining the structure of DNA, Watson and Crick remembered Pauling's successful endeavors in this domain. This retrieval was brought about by a basically verbal problem (i.e., determining the structure of DNA, or determining the structure of a complex molecule), which in turn led to a method, that may have been verbally formulated or perceptually based, involving a helix. Watson and Crick still had to decide on the exact structure of their helix, however, such as whether the bases should be positioned on the inside or outside. Selection of the first model's structure was based on perceptual processes, that is, both men saw problems with a base-inside model because of the varying sizes of the bases. In other words, they imagined the consequences of constructing the model in a certain way and then compared these consequences with what was known about the X-ray diffraction pattern produced by DNA. The same factors were involved when they modified the initial model in various ways so that it would not violate laws of chemistry.

To summarize, this case may have involved a complex intertwining of perceptual and verbal processes concerning both the retrieval of information from memory and the modification of early solutions through perceptual imagination and verbal reasoning. Again, however, the processes are not different from those already mentioned.

The brief discussion in Chapter 2 of Kekule's discovery of the benzene ring (six carbon atoms in a ring) raised questions about whether, as is usually assumed, his discovery occurred in a dream and if it involved his imagining snakes. The possibility was raised that both assumptions are false, and that Kekule's discovery probably came about as he imagined strings of atoms (however he represented them) while sitting lost in thought. Assuming that this is indeed how the discovery came about, then it too appears to be based on perceptual information and on the use of this information in imagination. Once Kekule imagined a string of atoms, it was not difficult to extend the imagination to moving strings in various configurations. This, is in turn, led to the ring structure that solved the problem.

This use of imagination is by no means limited to creative scientists of great ability. If I think of the ballet, for example, I imagine dancers in constant movement. Indeed, it is difficult for me to imagine dancers motionless for a significant amount of time. This may be the same sort of capacity as Kekule used. Thus, as several of the situations presented earlier demonstrated, creative thinking involves the use of imagination; such use is not particularly extraordinary, however, because we all have the capacity to imagine things.

In addition to the creative *solution* to a problem, one can also talk about the creative analysis or formulation of a problem, which involves approaching a problem in a different way from the approaches taken by others. Such analyses are thought to play an important role in science and the arts. In science, creative formulation is often cited as the first step in solving a previously unsolvable problem. In the arts, such formulation might involve the invention of a new art form that opened up a new avenue of expression. A more concrete example of such an analysis is presented in Chapter 4, concerning an engineer who, on examining the long loops in the tubules in human kidneys, concluded that the tubes functioned as part of a counter-current multiplier. As mentioned in Chapter 4, Edward deBono referred to this incident as an example of a creative way of looking at a problem. From my point of view, the analysis of this situation is the same as the analysis just presented, and involves the role of past experience in problem solving. The engineer recognized the similarity between kidney tubules and one type of engineering device because he had extensive experience with such devices and the configuration of the tubules resembled that of a counter-current multiplier. Thus, once again we have a situation in which previous knowledge is brought to bear on a new problem because the new situation is similar, though not identical, to the old.

Problem Solving in Art

These ideas also relate to artistic creativity, at least in some cases. For example, when an eighteenth century composer was commissioned to write a symphony, the problem was partly well-defined and partly ill-defined. Writing a symphony was partly well-defined because of the guidelines concerning the form a classical symphony should take. Writing a symphony was also ill-defined because the composer had to produce specific melodies and determine how they would be arranged for the orchestra.

Similarly, when Picasso accepted the commission to paint a mural for the Spanish pavilion at the 1937 world's fair the problem was primarily ill-defined. The bombing of Guernica gave him the stimulus for defining the problem more precisely, but he still had to decide exactly how to represent his message. By using his past experience as the basis for the solution of this problem, his new work was composed of symbols he had used before (the bull, the horse, a light-bearing woman, and so on), although the particular product was new. An interesting analogy can be drawn between Picasso's creation of *Guernica* and what a nonartist would do in the same situation. If asked to describe the bombing and its significance, a nonartist would use language, would take familiar words and combine them in novel ways in order to express the feelings aroused by the incident. A painter expresses feelings about an incident in a similar way through the use of visual symbols that he or she has developed over the course of a career; these visual symbols are modified as needed in order to deal with the specific event in question. Thus, Picasso's ability to produce something like *Guernica* is based, in part, on his previous development of a vocabulary of visual symbols, which can be used to tell a story. In addition he had to use his own judgment to determine when the mural conveyed what he intended it to.

In summary, the creation of a work like *Guernica,* which is not simply a realistic rendering of an event, may involve the artist's first developing a symbol system of sufficient generality that it can be applied to a new situation. The new work would involve using these symbols in ways that express the meaning the artist desires and the artist's conception of the meaning of the work would serve as the criterion for judging the adequacy of the work as it is produced.

As discussed in Chapter 7, Calder's mobiles grew out of his striving to express new experiences through the medium with which he was most comfortable, that is, wire sculpture. Calder had made objects out of wire when he was a child, and his later experiences at the circus led him to construct a circus of movable animals and people. The development of abstract movable sculptures evolved out of his combined exposure to realistic movable sculpture and Mondrian's abstract painting.

This case is both similar to and different from those already discussed. It differs because it did not involve the solution of a specific problem; that is, Calder was never faced with the specific problem of trying to make abstract sculpture. Rather, such pieces evolved as a natural development of his career as a sculptor. The commitment to a career as a sculptor (or perhaps any career), means that one constantly looks for new possibilities for one's work. Thus, when Calder came upon works of other artists, one of the ways he saw them was in terms of the possibilities they had for his own work. The Getzels and Csickszentmihalyi study of art students discussed in Chapter 7 emphasized "problem finding" as an important aspect in the development of an artist. Although I do not completely agree with their use of this concept, it seems a very apt description of what happens as an artist's interests change throughout his or her career, through outside influences and personal development. One could summarize by saying that a commitment to a career in sculpture is a commitment to a "problem-finding" orientation concerning sculpture, meaning that such an individual would examine all experiences from the point of view of his or her own way of doing things. Production of a new style, therefore, may be the result of a long-term commitment to working in a given area. Only in this way could enough small changes in the artist's work accumulate to produce a significant change.

This brief survey mentions only some of the many avenues of creativity. Poetry, literature, drama, musical composition, architecture, physics, and philosophy, etc. were not discussed. Given the differences involved in these domains, it seems reasonable to assume that many other sorts of psychological processes are involved in the creative thinking they entail and that one or two universally relevant thought processes are unlikely. This diversity of thought processes leads to the further conclusion that the psychological characteristics of creative individuals differ from one domain to the next. Furthermore, it is also true that the thought processes involved in these domains are those we all possess.

Is There Really Nothing Extraordinary About Creative Geniuses?

After questioning the concept of genius, the discussion in Chapter 5 concluded that there are no specific psychological characteristics upon which genius depends. First, the characteristics that are important for creative work depend on the specific area the individual is working in. Creativity in one area of physics may not depend on the same characteristics as creativity in another area, indicating that no small set of characteristics underlies creativity in all areas. Second, there is much evidence of inconsistent creative achievement in the careers of even the greatest scientists and artists. Assuming that one's personality characteristics remain basically the same for relatively long periods of one's life, this indicates that the same characteristics can play a role in an individual's producing works of genius and works of less merit. If so, then those characteristics cannot, in and of themselves, be the basis for creative achievement. Therefore, it may not even be correct to say that certain personality characteristics are *necessary* although not *sufficient,* for creative achievement. A given personality type may facilitate creative achievement only in relation to a specific problem, and then only within a specific environmental situation. As discussed in Chapter 5, the same personality characteristics which supposedly are necessary for creative achievement in one situation may actually interfere with creative achievement in another. Thus, whether or not certain characteristics could be called necessary for creative achievement becomes problematic. Finally, whether or not an individual is a genius depends on the judgment of posterity. Since an individual's reputation can change drastically over time, the same characteristics can produce works which are judged to be of genius and works of lesser merit. In addition, if it is true that all humans are capable of creativity in response to everyday problems, then all must possess whatever characteristics underlie creativity. We can conclude, therefore, that particularly creative individuals do not possess a unique set of characteristics and are not extraordinary individuals in this sense.

Even if we all possess the basic capacities which allow us to adapt to novel situations in our lives, that is, to be creative, such skills might differ from one individual to another. As a rough analogy, it is probably true that essentially all of us could learn to play tennis, but even after spending the same amount of time and energy practicing and playing, some of us would be better tennis players than others. Such basic differences between us in things like speed of certain reflexes, degree of hand-eye coordination, foot speed, and so on, would play a role in determining who would become the better tennis player. It must be emphasized, however, that these skills are domain-specific; that is, the skills needed for tennis might not be important in diving or wrestling. Therefore, talk of a general "athletic ability" that differs among individuals may not be correct.

A similar analysis also may apply to creative achievement. For example, we can all learn to draw, but an extremely good memory for visual detail may be necessary for a certain type of artistic creativity. If so, then the degree to which individuals differ in this capacity will result in differences in the potential for creative work in that area. Likewise, though we could all probably learn to play an instrument and also learn to compose, differences in things like auditory memory and/or auditory imagination (the ability to imagine sounds) may limit one's capacity to do creative work in the area. As still further examples, certain problems in physics may be solved by an individual who possesses extraordinary skills of visual imagination, while others might be solved by an individual who has an extraordinary ability to manipulate abstract symbols.

It should be emphasized once again that differences in such skills would not support the notion of creative genius, in the traditional sense, because the skills are not specific to creative thinking. The hypothetical skills of visual memory, auditory memory and imagination, visual imagination, and symbol manipulation are used in many different situations, those that require ordinary thinking and those traditionally associated with creative thinking. Of course, one of the basic assumptions of the present point of view is that the same thinking processes *are* involved in all sorts of situations, and no distinction should be made between the thinking processes involved in creativity and those involved elsewhere.

In addition to possible differences in skills of various sorts, it is also possible that truly creative individuals are extraordinary in terms of their motivation level. Biographical information and psychological studies of creative individuals show that the creative genius is totally committed to work. The most influential scientists and artists in modern Western culture have had long careers characterized by very high productivity. Freud, for example, produced 330 publications in a forty-five-year career, Picasso produced several thousand works in seventy-five years; Einstein, 248 publications in fifty-three years; and Darwin, 119 in fifty-one years. In order to produce such voluminous work, these individuals spent much more time working than ordinary individuals do. The degree of commitment to one's work might be an important difference between creative and noncreative individuals. High motivation alone, on the other hand, does not constitute scientific genius in the traditional sense because one could be highly motivated and produce a great deal of work without ever solving an important problem or having a lasting influence.

Another skill which may be related to motivational differences involves the ability to concentrate. Although no experimental evidence is available on this question, much anecdotal evidence supports the claim that creative individuals get so wrapped up in their work that they forget about the rest of the world. Such an example was discussed in Chapter 2, in which a scientist became so engrossed in his work that one morning he took two baths, one after the other, without realizing it. In any case, though it is not clear whether such depth of concentration occurs independently of the high motivation that characterizes creative individuals, it is not a skill specific to creativity since we all have the capacity to become totally absorbed in something if the situation is right.

These motivational differences may be important in several ways in influencing the quality of one's output. First of all, some situations require that the thinker go far beyond the initial situation before anything of value will result. An example of this might be the changes that had to occur in Darwin's thinking before he could develop the theory of evolution through natural selection. The degree of motivation becomes crucial in instances where such changes can only occur over relatively long periods of time. Secondly, if truly innovate work in a given field only comes about through extensive work involving much revision and the incorporation of new data, etc., the individual in question has to be highly motivated to sustain such effort. Finally, because the more motivated individual spends more time thinking about the problem, the probability of any chance occurrence being helpful is maximized. To summarize, motivational differences could result in significant differences in productivity and creativity among individuals despite the fact that similar thought processes are involved.

As this analysis of skills and motivation shows, one cannot attribute creative success solely to chance factors in an individual's life. Although it is true that chance factors may play a role (i.e., if Darwin's grandfather had not been interested in evolution, Charles might not have been either), these factors only apply to the specific individual involved. To continue this example, it is probably true that only someone of Darwin's temperament could have patiently sifted through such vast amounts of information for years and worked through the complicated reasoning process discussed in Chapter 6. This resulted in his abandoning his monad theory, which was almost directly based on accepted theory, and discovering a novel formulation that answered the question of how species evolved.

Though there may be some ways in which creative individuals are extraordinary when compared with the rest of the population, these differences may lie in very specific skills and their level of motivation rather than in a general creative capacity that could be called "creative genius." The extraordinarily creative individual may simply be extraordinarily good at whatever skill is required to do great work in a given domain. Once again, however, these extraordinary skills will not be relevant to every problem the individual works on, which means there will be cases in which the "genius" may produce merely ordinary work.

Creative Thinking is Inevitable

The genius view of creativity sees creative thinking as an extraordinary event that demands explanation. Creative thinking demands explanation because it is assumed that humans are not required to think creatively in the ordinary course of events. Ordinary life is assumed to involve a trivial series of familiar events that can be addressed without resorting to creative thinking. It is only in extraordinary circumstances, so this line of reasoning goes, that creative thinking becomes necessary. These are the circumstances that bring out the best in human thinking, and this is the thinking that needs an explanation.

If one takes a slightly different view of the demands of ordinary familiar situations, however, one comes to a very different conclusion concerning the nature of creative thinking and its relationship to "ordinary" thinking. One also comes to a very different appreciation of what ordinary thinking entails.

The ancient Greek philosopher Heraclitus believed that the only constant aspect of the world was that everything constantly changed. He summarized this in the well-known saying that one can never step into the same river twice. This is true because the river is constantly changing.

By the same token, one could say that no two experiences are ever identical. Even if one does "the same thing" more than once, on close examination the experiences will be different. As one picks up a pencil in order to start writing, for example, the position of one's hand, the pencil, and the paper all change from one time to the next. Furthermore, if one considers more complicated actions such as getting dressed, taking a shower, cooking a meal, or starting a car the room for variability becomes much more obvious. Thus, let us assume for the sake of discussion that human beings (and probably all complex organisms) never do the same thing twice. Taken seriously, this assumption has far-ranging implications for our conception of creative thinking.

If humans never produce the same response twice, then novelty, and hence creativity, are the norm and the thought processes involved in producing novelty are always being used. To put it another way, there may be no thinking except creative thinking, since our ordinary functioning involves successful adaptation to novel situations, and thus meets the criteria for creativity. There are two facets to this "ordinary creativity:" perception and response. As far as perception is concerned, if nothing remains the same, then there is never an exact match between the situation and one's knowledge. Response to a situation, therefore, must be based on a partial match between that situation and what one knows. The ability to respond in this way is the basis for our capacity to deal with novelty and, thus, is central to our creative thinking ability. It is also central to our thinking activities in situations not normally acknowledged as requiring creativity, however, which once again points to the uniformity of all thinking.

As regards response, if the environment is never constant, the individual's response will never exactly fit the present situation, no matter how closely based on past experience. After a response has been called forth, therefore, modification will invariably be required. Thus, no two responses will ever be exactly alike because no two situations will be exactly alike. In conclusion, because novel output can be considered normal, the question again arises whether a distinction can be made between the creative and noncreative.

In existing psychological theories, this idea is not as novel as it may appear to be in discussions of creativity. First of all, psychologists have long known that once an organism learned to respond to one situation, it could produce that response in other situations. This phenomenon is called "stimulus generalization" because the learning is "generalized" to stimuli that were not originally involved. It was also noted that learned responses could often be changed in response to environmental changes. This was called response generalization. The only difference between the notions of stimulus and response generalization and my point of view is that, from my perspective, explicit notions of generalization are only needed if one assumes initially that the same stimulus conditions usually repeat themselves. If one makes this assumption, then stimulus generalization and response generalization are brought forth to explain how organisms are able to respond when there is no repetition. I believe this is unnecessarily complicated. If one assumes first that no environmental situation ever repeats, then stimulus and response generalization always occur and no special mechanisms are needed. Thus, a small shift in emphasis results in a large change in the simplicity of theorizing. Though we are still left with the task of explaining ordinary behavior, we are at a great advantage because we now must explain only one sort of behavior.

This same sort of analysis can be seen in the theorizing of Jean Piaget, who used the concepts of assimilation and accommodation to explain the adaptation of organisms to constantly changing events. According to Piaget's view, the first step in dealing with any event is *assimilating* that event to one's knowledge, that is, trying to match that event as closely as possible to what one knows. One must then *accommodate* one's response to the novel aspects of the event, thereby producing a novel response which is adapted to the new situation. It should be noted that Piaget explicitly tried to deal with adaptation to the novel as the ordinary course of events, rather than assuming there is some constancy in the environment. It is also interesting to note that Piaget wrote the forward to Howard Gruber's book on Darwin, which served as the basis for much of the discussion in Chapter 6.

If one accepts the basic principle that the environment is constantly changing, then much of the mystery surrounding creativity is removed in a single stroke. It follows from this assumption that all behavior involves novelty at its core, which renders meaningless any distinction between the creative and the noncreative.

Creativity and Myth

I began with the wish to clear up some of the mystery surrounding creative thinking and creative individuals, and the discussion has been directed toward that end. I have shown, on the one hand, that much of the genius view of creativity, which is full of mystery, is remarkably fragile and will not withstand critical analysis. Furthermore, the genius view may be based on a fundamental misconception concerning the presence of originality in human thinking. The incremental point of view, on the other hand, developed from an analysis of simple problem solving and has been very useful in organizing a large body of work collected from studies of scientific and artistic creativity. This book serves only as an introduction to this topic and cannot address all of the important questions. Indeed, I have explicitly talked about a "framework" or a "point of view" throughout the book in order to make clear that nothing like a theory of creativity is being presented here. However, given the large increases in our knowledge over the last decade or so, and the general consensus that seems to have developed among cognitive psychologists, a theory of creative thinking may not be too far away.

REFERENCE NOTES

Chapter 1

Page 1 Muses: see any edition of Bulfinch's *Mythology* (e.g., 1959). Hecht quote: *New York Times,* 23 January 1983, p. 33. Studies of famous scientists: Hadamard (1954).

Page 2 Shakespeare article: Mitgang (1985). Article on "Genius mind": Briggs (1984).

Page 2 Watson's view on creativity: Watson (1958, p. 247).

Pages 4-6 Novel use of an object: Koestler (1964); Perkins (1981, Ch. 3).

Page 6 Candle problem: Duncker (1945).

Pages 6-9 Use of protocols: in chess—DeGroot (1966); in poetry—Patrick (1935), Perkins (1981, Ch. 1); in candle problem—Weisberg & Suls (1973, Exp. III). Further discussion of candle problem: Weisberg (1980, Chap. 10).

Pages 9-11 Charlie problem: Weisberg & DiCamillo (1985).

Pages 12-13 Expertise in chess: DeGroot (1966), Chase & Simon (1973).

Page 13 Expertise in various areas: See summary in Mayer (1983, Chaps. 13-14).

Pages 13-14 Expertise and creativity: Greeno (1980).

Chapter 2

Page 15 Poincaré's theory: Poincaré (1913); Hadamard (1954); Koestler (1964); Freud (1913).

Page 16 Poincaré quotes: "ideas rose in clouds . . ."—Ghiselin (1952, p. 36).

Page 17 "The incidents of travel . . ."—Ghiselin (1952, p. 37).

Page 17 "A manifest sign of . . ."—Ghiselin (1952, p. 38).

Page 17 Mozart quote: "When I feel well . . ."—Ghiselin (1952, pp. 44-45).

Pages 17-18 Coleridge report: Coleridge (1816). Coleridge quote: Ghiselin (1952, pp. 84-85). Creativity and altered states of consciousness—see, e.g., Hadamard (1954).

Pages 18-19 Jumping the gap: Perkins (1981, Chap. 2).

Page 19   Believing the reports: See also Perkins (1981, Chap. 1).
Distortion in recall: Bartlett (1932); Bransford (1979).

Pages 19–20   Stages: Wallas (1926).
Preparation: see also Ghiselin (1952, Introduction); Hadamard (1954); Poincaré (1913)

Pages 20–21   Glimpse into the unconscious: Poincaré (1913); see, e.g., also Hadamard (1954).
Esthetic basis for judgment: Poincaré (1913); Koestler (1964).

Page 22   Gutenberg: see Koestler (1964).

Page 22   Bisociation: Koestler (1964, p. 119).

Pages 22–23   Freudian unconscious and creativity: Freud (1938); Kris (1952). Dreaming and bisociation: Koestler (1964, p. 178).

Pages 23–24   Automatic processing of meaning: Marcel (1983).
Well-learned skills: Shiffrin & Schneider (1977).
Automatic storage of information in memory: Hasker & Zacks (1979).

Page 24   Original use of "incubation": Wallas (1926); Poincaré (1913); Hadamard (1954).
Incubation simply as time away from a problem: Adams (1979, pp. 47–48).
Creative worrying: Olton (1979).

Page 25   Artists and poets: Patrick (1935, 1937).
Creative worrying again: Olton (1979).
Wallas's stages: Wallas (1926)
Eindhoven & Vinacke (1952).

Pages 25–26   Olton's studies: Olton (1979); Olton & Johnson (1976).

Pages 26–27   Read & Bruce (1982).
Study of spontaneous recalls: Gruneberg, Smith, & Rinfrow (1973).

Page 27   Mozart never wrote the letter: Anderson (1966); Deutsch (1964).
History of the letter: Deutsch (1964).
Mozart's compositional process: Einstein (1945, Chap. 8).
Mozart's memory: Sloboda (1984).

Pages 27–28   Schneider (1953).

Pages 28–29   Maier (1930).

Page 29   Creative worrying again: Olton (1979).
Poincaré's work habits: Poincaré (1913).

Page 30   Teeple's baths: Hadamard (1954, p. 35) Interestingly, a number of individuals have interpreted Teeple's two baths as evidence for *unconscious* thought processes (e.g., Hadamard, 1954; Glass, Holyoak, & Santa, 1979). That is, it is assumed that Teeple was doing his chemistry while unaware of it, since he took two baths. It seems to me that this interpretation is exactly backwards; Teeple was so consciously wrapped up in his chemistry that he barely could think about other things, and so he took two baths, without thinking.

Page 30   Patrick (1935, 1937).
Eindhaven & Vinacke (1952).

Wallas (1926).

Weak evidence for incubation from lab studies: Olton (1979); Read & Bruce (1982).

Pages 30-31   Alternative accounts of incubation: Woodworth & Schlossberg (1954, Chap. 26).

Page 31   Creativity in dreams: Hadamard (1954, p. 6).

Page 32   Importance of Kekule's dream: quote from Koestler (1964, p. 118).

Page 32   "Halbschlaf" and "Let us learn to dream . . .": Kekule quoted in Rothenberg (1979, pp. 395-6).

Page 33   This interpretation of Kekule's dream was suggested to me by Mason Spencer.

Chapter 3

Page 35   "Aha!" problems: Gardner (1978).

Page 36   Gardner quote: Gardner (1978, pp. vi–vii).

Page 37   "Nothing new": Watson (1958).
Thorndike's research: Thorndike (1913).

Page 37   Gestalt view in general: Wertheimer (1959).

Page 38   "Aha!" reactions in apes: Köhler (1976).
Working out of solution through perceptual processes: see also Duncker (1926).

Pages 38-40   Productive thinking in children: Wertheimer (1959, Ch. 1).

Pages 40-41   Perception and problem solving: Wertheimer (1959, Ch. 1).

Page 42   Gestalt acknowledgment of importance of knowledge: Wertheimer (1959, pp. 58–65).

Pages 42-43   Problem solving set: Luchins & Luchins (1959).

Pages 44-46   Testing fixation: Burnham & Davis (1969); Weisberg & Alba (1981).
Solution in a flash: Gardner (1978, p. vii).
Solution smoothly produced: Wertheimer (1959, p. 47ff).

Page 46   Köhler's apes and past experience: Birch (1945).

Pages 46-47   Learning sets: Harlow (1949).

Chapter 4

Pages 53-55   Quotes: DeBono (1968, p. 2, 3, 5); Adams (1979, p. 7); Gordon (1961, p. 3, 35); Watzlawick et al., (1974, p. xiii).

Pages 55-56   Guilford's theorizing: Guilford (1950, 1959).

Pages 57-59   Conceptual blockbusting: Adams (1979).

Page 59   "Esoteric psychologies": Ornstein (1973).

Page 59   Brainstorming: Osborn (1953).

Page 60   "Copious ideation": Osborn (1953, p. 146).

Page 60   Rules of brainstorming: Osborn (1953, Ch. VII).

Page 61   Osborn's evidence for brainstorming: Osborn (1953, pp. 90–95).

Pages 62–64   Group versus individual performance: Dunnette, Campbell, & Jastaad (1963); Bouchard & Hare (1970); Dillon, Graham, & Aidells (1972); Bouchard (1971).

Pages 64–66   Deferring judgment vs. voicing criticism: Weisskopf-Joelson & Eliseo (1961); Brilhart & Jochem (1964); Johnson, Parrott, & Stratton, (1964); Gerlach et al. (1966).

Page 67   Studies of creativity in laboratory problems: Perkins (1981, Ch. 2); Weisberg (1980, Ch. 10, 12); Weisberg & Alba (1981). Scientific discoveries: Darwin's notebooks— Gruber (1981); DNA—Watson (1968).
Relationship between divergent thinking and scientific creativity: see Busse & Mansfield (1981, Chap. 2).

Page 68   Example of divergent thinking: DeBono (1968, pp. 148–149).

Chapter 5

Pages 70–72   Measures of personality: study of values (Allport, 1965, Ch. 18); MMPI and other inventories (Megargee, 1972).

Pages 73–75   Core characteristics of genius: sensitivity to problems—Guilford (1950); description of Rutherford: Cline (1962, p. 19), Einstein & Infeld (1938, p. 92); artists' openness to emotion—Barron & Harrington (1981).

Page 75   Barron quote: Barron (1955, p. 478).

Pages 76–77   Mackinnon (1962).

Pages 79–80   Getzels & Csikszentmihalyi (1976).

Pages 81–83   All the examples, except Einstein: Broad (1983).
Einstein's letter to Born: Clark (1984, p. 414); Pais (1982, p. 443).
"Old museum piece": Clark (1984, p. 648).

Pages 83–84   Leonardo's notebooks: Taylor (1960).

Page 84   Dennis (1966).

Page 85   Bach's posthumous reputation: Wolff, et al. (1983, pp. 167–177).

Page 86   Forkel quote: Wolff, et al. (1983, pp. 169–170).

Page 87   Artist exercising degree of control: Getzels & Csikszentmihalyi (1976).

Chapter 6

Page 89   Description of Watson & Crick: Adams (1979, pp. 61–62).

Page 90   Lack of education: quote from DeBono (1968, p. 27).

Pages 91–98   Discussion of double helix: Judson (1979); Watson (1968).

Page 96   Watson quote: Watson (1968, pp. 123–125).

Page 97   Description of Franklin: Judson (1979).

Pages 98–99   Theory of evolution as leap: Rothenberg (1979, p. 104). Quote from Darwin: Gruber (1981, pp. 172–173).

Pages 98–105   Discussion of historical background of Darwin's work: Eiseley (1961). Discussion of Darwin's theorizing and notebooks: Gruber (1981).

Pages 104–105   Notebook entry concerning Malthus: Gruber (1981, p. 170).

Page 106   Reports by scientists concerning leaps of insight: see Hadamard (1954); Rothenberg (1979).

Chapter 7

Page 108   Self-reports: Ghiselin (1952). Mental disturbances: Prentky (1981).

Pages 111–113   Discussion of Calder: Calder (1966); Lipman (1972); Sweeney (1943).

Pages 113–115   Collage: Vallentin (1963, pp. 124–125); Daix (1965, pp. 90–93). For a somewhat different analysis of this development, see Cooper & Tinterow –1983, p. 84).

Page 116   Exhibit of poets' first drafts: Mitgang (1984). Perkins's study and quote: Perkins (1981, pp. 66–69).

Pages 117–118   Discussion of *The idiot:* Boell (1983). Dostoyevsky quote: Miller (1981, p. 49). Plans for first part of *The idiot,* and quotes: Wasiolek (1967; pp. 37–46, p. 80). second part: "under my pen"—Mochulsky (1967, p. 344); Prince as Christ—Wasiolek (1967, pp. 167, 168, 198).

Pages 118–120   Discussion of *Crime and punishment:* Hackenberg (1983). Discussion of Fitzgerald: Tatham (1983). Stevenson: Finch (1958).

Pages 120–121   Eindhoven & Vinacke (1952).

Pages 121–122   Getzels & Csikszentmihalyi (1976)

Pages 122–126   Discussions of *Guernica:* Arnheim, (1962); Blunt (1969).

Pages 126–128   Sources for *Guernica:* see especially Blunt (1969).

Pages 128–130   Beethoven's notebooks on the *Ninth Symphony:* Solomon (1977, Ch. 22).

Page 131   Bach's life: see Wolff, et al. (1983).

Page 132   Rules of composition: Buelow (1980); Marshall (1972). Bach the borrower: Carrell (1967).

Page 133   Borrowing in Handel: see Dean (1982); in Mozart: see Baker (1982) and Wollenberg, (1975); in Beethoven: see Derr (1984); in Haydn: Butterworth (1977).

Pages 134–135   Hayes (1981, Chap. 10).

Page 135   Composers' training: Einstein (1945, Ch. 8); Butterworth (1977, Ch. 2 & 3); Baker (1982).

Page 136   Blunt quote: Blunt (1969, p. 2).

Chapter 8

Pages 139–141   Well- versus ill-defined problems: Weisberg (1980, pp. 270–272).

Page 143   Problem finding: Getzels & Csikszentmihalyi (1976).

Page 145   Productivity of creative individuals: Simonton (1984, Chap. 5).

Page 147   Stimulus and response generalization: see, e.g., Hintzman (1978, Chap. 4).

Page 148   Piaget—assimilation and accommodation: Weisberg (1980, Chap. 13).

BIBLIOGRAPHY

Adams, J. L. (1979). *Conceptual blockbusting.* 2d ed. New York: Norton.

Allport, G. W. (1965). *Pattern and growth in personality.* New York: Holt, Rinehart, Winston.

Anderson, E. (1966). *The letters of Mozart and his family.* 2d ed. New York: St. Martin's Press.

Arnheim, R. (1962). *Picasso's Guernica: The genesis of a painting.* Berkeley: University of California Press.

Baker, R. (1982). *Mozart.* London: Thames and Hudson.

Barron, F. (1955). The disposition towards originality. *Journal of Abnormal and Social Psychology, 51,* 478–485.

Barron, F., & Harrington, D. M. (1981). Creativity, intelligence, and personality. *Annual Reviews of Psychology, 32,* 439–476.

Bartlett, F. C. (1932). *Remembering.* Cambridge, England: Cambridge University Press.

Birch, H. (1975). The relation of previous experience to insightful problem solving. *Journal of Comparative Psychology, 38,* 367–383.

Blunt, A. (1969). *Picasso's "Guernica."* New York: Oxford University Press.

Boell, J. (1983). Dostoyevsky and the creative process in *The Idiot.* Unpublished manuscript, Temple University.

Bouchard, T. J., Jr. (1971). Whatever happened to brainstorming? *Journal of Creative Behavior, 5,* 182–189.

Bouchard, T. J., Jr., & Hare, M. (1970). Size, performance, and potential in brainstorming groups. *Journal of Applied Psychology, 54,* 51–55.

Bransford, J. (1979). *Human cognition. Learning, understanding and remembering.* Belmont, CA: Wadsworth.

Briggs, J. (1984). The genius mind. *Science Digest, 92,* 74–78.

Brillhart, J. K., & Jochem, L. M. (1964). Effects of different patterns on outcomes of problem-solving discussions. *Journal of Applied Psychology, 48,* 175–179.

Broad, W. J. (1983). What happens when heroes of science go astray? *New York Times,* February 1, pp. C1–C2.

Buelow, G. J. (1980). Rhetoric and music. In S. Sadie (Ed.) *The new Grove dictionary of music and musicians.*

Bullfinch, T. (1959). *Mythology.* (E. Fuller, ed.) New York, Dell.

Burnham, C. A., & Davis, K. G. (1969). The 9-dot problem: beyond perceptual organization. *Psychonomic Science, 17,* 321–323.

Butterworth, N. (1977). *Haydn, his life and times.* Tunbridge Wells, Kent, England: Midas Books.

Calder, A. (1966). *Calder, an autobiography with pictures.* New York: Pantheon Books.

Carrell, N. (1967). *Bach the borrower.* London: George Allen & Unwin.

Chase, W. G., & Simon, H. A. (1973). Perception in chess. *Cognitive Psychology, 4,* 55–81.

Clark, R. W. (1984). *Einstein: The life and times.* New York: Avon Books.

Cline, B. L. (1962). *Men who made a new physics.* New York: Signet Books.

Coleridge, S. T. (1816). *Prefatory note to Kubla Khan.* In B. Ghiselin (Ed.) *The creative process.* New York: Mentor, pp. 84–85.

Cooper, D., & Tinterow, G. (1983). The essential cubism, 1907–1920. New York: Braziller.

Daix, P. (1965). *Picasso.* New York: Praeger.

Dean, W. (1982). *The New Grove Handel.* New York: Norton.

DeBono, E. (1968). *New think.* New York: Basic Books.

DeGroot, A. (1966). Perception and memory versus thought: some old ideas and recent findings. In B. Kleinmuntz (ed.) *Problem Solving: Research, method, and theory.* New York: John Wiley, pp. 19–50.

Dennis, W. (1966). Creative productivity between the ages of 20 and 80 years. *Science, 123,* 724–725.

Derr, E. (1984). Beethoven's long-term memory of C.P.E. Bach's rondo in E-flat, W. 61/1 (1787), manifest in the variations in E-flat for piano, opus 35 (1802). *Musical Quarterly, 70,* 45–76.

Deutsch, O. E. (1964). Spurious Mozart letters. *Music Review, 25,* 120–123.

Dillon, P. C., Graham, W. K., & Aidells, A. L. (1972). Brainstorming on a "hot" problem: Effects of training and practice on individual and group performance. *Journal of Applied Psychology, 56,* 487–490.

Duncker, K. (1926). A qualitative (experimental and theoretical) study of productive thinking (solving of comprehensible problems). *Pedagogical Seminar, 33,* 642–708.

Duncker, K. (1945). On problem-solving. *Psychological Monographs, 58,* No. 5, Whole No. 270.

Dunnette, M. D., Campbell, J., & Jastaad, K. (1963). The effects of group participation on brainstorming effectiveness for two industrial samples. *Journal of Applied Psychology, 47,* 10–37.

Eindhoven, J. E., & Vinacke, W. E. (1952). Creative processes in painting. *The Journal of General Psychology, 47,* 139–164.

Einstein, Albert, & Infeld, L. (1938). *The evolution of physics.* New York: Simon & Schuster.

Einstein, Alfred (1945). *Mozart: His character, his work.* London: Oxford University Press.

Eiseley, L. (1961). *Darwin's century. Evolution and the men who discovered it.* New York: Anchor Books.

Finch, H. R. (1958). Introduction. In R. L. Stevenson, *Kidnapped.* New York: Washington Square Press.

Freud, S. (1938). *The interpretation of dreams.* New York: Modern Library.

Gardner, M. (1978). *Aha! Insight.* New York: Freeman.

Gerlach, V. S., Schutz, R. E., Baker, R. L., & Mazer, G. E. (1964). Effects of variations in test directions on originality test response. *Journal of Educational Psychology, 55,* 79–83.

Getzels, J., & Csikszentmihalyi, M. (1976). *The creative vision: A longitudinal study of problem finding in art.* New York: John Wiley.

Ghiselin, B. (Ed.) (1952). *The creative process.* New York: Mentor.

Glass, A. L., Holyoak, K. J., & Santa, J. L. (1979). *Cognition.* Reading, MA: Addison-Wesley.

Gordon, W. J. J. (1961). *Synectics.* New York: Collier.

Guilford, J. P. (1950). Creativity. *American Psychologist, 5,* 444–454.

Guilford, J. P. (1959). Traits of creativity. In H. H. Anderson (ed.) *Creativity and its cultivation.* New York: Harper, pp. 142–161.

Greeno, J. G. (1980). Trends un the theory of knowledge for problem solving. In D. T. Tuma, & R. Reif (eds.) *Problem solving and education: Issues in teaching and learning.* Hillsdale, NJ: Erlbaum.

Gruber, H. (1981). *Darwin on man.* 2d ed. Chicago: University of Chicago Press.

Gruneberg, M., Smith, R., & Rinfrow, P. (1973). An investigation into response blockaging. *Acta Psychologica, 37,* 187–196.

Hackenberg, T. (1983). *Dostoyevsky's Crime and punishment: A creative masterpiece?* Unpublished manuscript, Temple University.

Hadamard, J. (1954). *The psychology of invention in the mathematical field.* New York: Dover.

Harlow, H. (1949). The formation of learning sets. *Psychological Review, 56,* 51–65.

Hasher, L. A., & Zacks, R. T. (1979). Automatic and effortful processes in memory. *Journal of Experimental Psychology: General, 108,* 365–388.

Hayes, J. R. (1981). *The complete problem solver.* Philadelphia: Franklin Institute Press.

Hintzman, D. L. (1978). *The psychology of learning and memory.* New York: Freeman.

Johnson, D. M., Parrott, G. L., & Stratton, R. P. (1968). Production and judgment of solutions to five problems. *Journal of Educational Psychology Monograph Supplement, 59,* No. 6, Part 2.

Judson, H. F. (1979). *The eighth day of creation: Makers of the revolution in biology.* New York: Simon & Schuster.

Koestler, A. (1964). *The act of creation.* New York: Macmillan.

Köhler, W. (1976). *The mentality of apes.* New York: Liveright.

Lipman, J. (ed.) (1972). *Calder's circus.* New York: Dutton.

Luchins, A. S., & Luchins, E. H. (1959). *Rigidity of behavior.* Eugene, OR: University of Oregon Press.

Mackinnon, D. W. (1962). The personality correlates of creativity: a study of American architects. In G. S. Nielsen (ed.), *Proceedings of the 14th International Congress of Applied Psychology,* Vol. 2, Copenhagen: Munksgaard, 11–39.

Maier, N. R. F. (1931). Reasoning in humans: II. The solution of a problem and its appearance in consciousness. *Journal of Comparative Psychology, 12,* 181–194.

Mansfield, R. S., & Busse, T. V. (1981). *The psychology of creativity and discovery.* Chicago: Nelson-Hall.

Marcel, A. J. (1983). Conscious and unconscious perception: experiments on visual masking and word recognition. *Cognitive Psychology, 15,* 197–237.

Marshall, R. L. (1972). *The compositional process of J. S. Bach: A study of the autograph scores of the vocal works,* 2 vols. Princeton, NJ: Princeton University Press.

Mayer, R. E. (1983). *Thinking, problem solving, cognition.* New York: Freeman.

Megargee, E. I. (1972). *The CPI handbook.* San Francisco: Jossey Bass.

Miller, R. F. (1981). *Dostoyevsky and The Idiot: Author, narrator, and reader.* Cambridge, MA: Harvard University Press.

Mitgang, H. (1984). Library displays the poet's search for perfection. *New York Times,* January 3, p. 21.

Mitgang, H. (1985). 'Sblood! Still feuding over the bard. *New York Times,* February 9, p. 9.

Mochulsky, K. (1967). *Dostoyevsky: His life and work.* (M. A. Minihan, trans.) Princeton, NJ: Princeton University Press.

Mozart, J. C. W. A. (1964). A letter. Reprinted in B. Ghiselin (Ed.) *The creative process.* New York: Mentor, pp. 44–45.

Olton, R. M. (1979). Experimental studies of incubation: Searching for the elusive. *Journal of Creative Behavior, 13,* 9–22.

Olton, R. M., & Johnson, D. M. (1976). Mechanisms of incubation in creative problem solving. *American Journal of Psychology, 89,* 617–630.

Ornstein, R. (Ed.) (1973). *The nature of human consciousness: A book of readings.* San Francisco: Freeman.

Osborn, A. (1953). *Applied imagination.* Revised edition. New York: Charles Scribner's Sons.

Pais, A. (1982). *"Subtle is the Lord . . ." The science and the life of Albert Einstein.* Oxford, England: Oxford University Press.

Patrick, C. (1935). Creative thought in poets. In R. Woodworth (ed.), *Archives of Psychology, 178.*

Patrick, C. (1937). Creative thought in artists. *Journal of Psychology, 4,* 35–73.

Perkins, D. (1981). *The mind's best work.* Cambridge, MA: Harvard University Press.

Poincaré, H. (1913). Mathematical creation. In *The foundations of science.* (Translated by G. B. Halsted). New York: The Science Press. Reprinted in B. Ghiselin (ed.) (1952). *The creative process.* New York: New American Library.

Prentky, R. A. (1981). *Creativity and psychopathology.* New York: Praeger.

Read, J. D., & Bruce, D. (1982). Longitudinal tracking of difficult memory retrievals. *Cognitive Psychology, 14,* 280–300.

Rothenberg, A. (1979). *The emerging goddess.* Chicago: University of Chicago Press.

Schneider, E. (1953). *Coleridge, opium, and Kubla Khan.* Chicago: University of Chicago Press.

Shiffrin, R. M., & Schneider, W. (1977). Controlled and automatic human information processing. II. Perceptual learning, automatic attending, and a general theory. *Psychological Review, 84,* 127–190.

Simonton, D. K. (1984). *Genius, creativity, and leadership.* Cambridge, MA: Harvard University Press.

Sloboda, J. (1984). *The musical mind.* New York: Oxford University Press.

Solomon, M. (1977). *Beethoven.* New York: Schirmer Books.

Sweeney, J. J. (1943). *Alexander Calder.* New York: Museum of Modern Art.

Tatham, T. (1983). The composition of *Tender is the night.* Unpublished manuscript, Temple University.

Taylor, P. (Ed.) (1960). *The notebooks of Leonardo da Vinci.* New York: New American Library.

Thorndike, E. L. (1911). *Animal intelligence.* New York: Macmillan.

Vallentin, A. (1963). *Picasso.* Garden City, NY: Doubleday.

Wallas, G. (1926). *The art of thought.* New York: Harcourt Brace.

Wasiolek, E. (Ed.) (1967). *The notebooks for the Idiot.* (K. Strelsky, trans.). Chicago: University of Chicago Press.

Watson, J. (1968). *The double helix.* New York: Signet.

Watson, J. B. (1958). *Behaviorism.* Chicago: University of Chicago Press.

Watzlawick, P., Weakland, J., & Fisch, R. (1974). *Change. Principles of problem formation and problem resolution.* New York: Norton.

Weisberg, R. W. (1980). *Memory, thought, and behavior.* New York: Oxford University Press.

Weisberg, R. W., & Alba, J. W. (1981). An examination of the alleged role of "fixation" in the solution of several "insight" problems. *Journal of Experimental Psychology: General, 110,* 169–192.

Weisberg, R. W., & DiCamillo, M. A. (1985). Multiple memory searches as the basis for restructuring in an insight problem. Unpublished paper, Temple University.

Weisberg, R. W., & Suls, J. (1973). An information-processing model of Duncker's candle problem. *Cognitive Psychology, 4,* 255–276.

Weisskopf-Joelson, E., & Eliseo, T. S. (1961). An experimental study of the effectiveness of brainstorming. *Journal of Applied Psychology, 45,* 45–49.

Wertheimer, M. (1959). *Productive thinking.* New York: Harper & Row.

Wolff, C., Emery, W., Helm, E., Jones, R., Warburton, E., & Derr, E. S. (1983). *The New Grove Bach Family.* New York: Norton.

Wollenberg, S. (1975). The Jupiter theme: new light on its creation. *Musical Times, 66,* 781–783.

Woodworth, R. S., & Schlossberg, H. (1954). *Experimental psychology.* New York: Holt, Rinehart and Winston.

Name Index

Subject Index